Strengthen Your Faith
(Six Key Questions)

Analyzing Some Tough Issues to Help Christians Deepen Their Faith and Their Joy

Richard B. Ramsay

Strengthen Your Faith (Six Key Questions);
Analyzing Some Tough Issues to Help Christians Deepen Their
Faith and Their Joy

Richard B. Ramsay

ISBN: 979-8-90148-585-9
Staten House

Published previously as *Strengthen Your Faith; Analyzing Some Tough Issues to Help Christians Deepen Their Faith and Their Joy*

Published in 2020 in Spanish by *Publicaciones Faro de Gracia* as *Fortalece tu fe; reflexiones para resolver algunas dudas comunes*.

All Bible passages are quoted from the *English Standard Version* (ESV, Crossway Bibles, 2016), taken from *Logos Bible Study Software*, unless otherwise indicated.

CONTENTS

Preface

One of my favorite short stories is called "The Switchman," written by Juan José Arreola, from Mexico. A traveler arrives at a train station, with his suitcase in hand and a ticket to a place called "T." An old man with a small red lantern, who later identifies himself as a retired switchman, taps him on the shoulder, and they begin a bizarre dialogue about the railway system. He explains that, while they have nice trains, you can't really count on them to be on time. He recommends renting a room in the nearby hotel for a month while he waits. In fact, even if you happen to catch a train, he says, it might not take you to your desired destination. Some people ride around for years and finally decide to get off and build a new colony in some remote location, and others just stay on board until they die.[1]

Without God, life can seem unpredictable and absurd, like this story. Even as Christians, life can be surprisingly difficult to understand. But it helps enormously to believe in a truly sovereign God who loves us and takes care of us.

Abraham obeyed God's call and headed for Canaan with his whole family, "not knowing where he was going" (Hebrews 11:8). Abraham wasn't just wandering around aimlessly. He knew he was going to Canaan, but he didn't know what the journey would be like, nor the details of where they would be living. He just knew God was with them. Hebrews also tells us that "he was looking forward to the city that has foundations, whose designer and builder is God" (11:10).

---

[1] Juan José Arreola, "El guardagujas", in *Antología de Cuentos Hispanoamericanos*, ed. Mario Rodríguez Fernández (Santiago, Chile: Editorial Universitaria, 1998), 235-242.

For Christians, our story is very different from "The Switchman." Unlike the uncertain traveler, we can be sure that we will arrive at our final destination. God built the railroad and the trains, He is the switchman and the conductor, and He has prepared a beautiful eternal place for us. We don't know the details of the journey, but if we trust the Lord, we don't need to know them. Instead of being confused and frightened, we can look at life as an adventure.

We often analyze things from our own personal human point of view, without considering the divine perspective. In this case we are like passengers on a train in the valley below, watching the trees fly by, uncertain what we will find around the next curve. But we can also climb up the mountain to see the bigger picture. It encourages us when we can see the beautiful hills, rivers, lakes and the final destination from above.

After Joseph was sold by his own brothers and taken to Egypt as a slave, he was able to help many people through a time of drought and hunger. Later, when he met his brothers again, his response revealed a dual perspective, "As for you, you meant evil against me, but God meant it for good, to bring it about that many people should be kept alive, as they are today" (Genesis 50:20). He was able to see the divine plan.

The purpose of this book is to help you climb up to get a better view, to help you grow in your faith and enjoy the journey. I want to deal with the following questions: 1) Can I lose my salvation? 2) How can I experience the fullness of the Holy Spirit? 3) How should we use the Old Testament laws today? 4) How can I avoid spiritual dryness? 5) If God is in control of all things and plans all things, in what sense do I have free will? 6) Why does God allow us to suffer?

These matters are extremely practical, but they are also complex theological issues. They are questions I myself have wrestled with during my whole life, topics that I continue to analyze. I want to share the results of my reflection and Bible study, with the hope that it might be helpful for you.

The book is meant for Christians who already understand the basic doctrines of the gospel and are wrestling with some of these deeper issues. The apostle Paul says we should not be spiritual "children," "carried about by every wind of doctrine" (Ephesians 4:14).

I am convinced that to grow in Christ and to enjoy our life in relationship with God, we need a deeper understanding of His grace, the theme that unifies the reflections in this book. Peter calls on us to "grow in the grace and knowledge of our Lord and Savior Jesus Christ" (2 Peter 3:18). Paul urges us to "continue in the grace of God" (Acts 13:43), instead of falling back into our natural default of depending on our own strength.

Questions for review are included in each chapter, as well as suggestions for Bible study, memorization, prayer, reflection and discussion. You might consider using the book for group study.

The Author

Dr. Ramsay was a missionary in Chile for 21 years, teaching in a seminary and planting churches. There he met his wife, Angelica. They now live in Florida. They have two children, both married. For the past 25 years, they have worked internationally in distance education, traveling to teach classes and producing resources for theological education and leadership training. Richard has taught for *Universidad FLET* and *Thirdmill Seminary* and has developed many online courses.

He holds a D.Min. degree and an M.Div. from *Westminster Theological Seminary*, as well as a Th.M. from *Covenant Theological Seminary*.

Other books by the author include *The Certainty of the Faith, Am I Good Enough?, Basic Greek and Exegesis, Intellectual Integrity, Catholics and Protestants, Transformed into the Image of Jesus, Synopsis of the Bible, Putting the Pieces Together,* and *Orientation for Leaders.*

Dedication

I would like to dedicate this book to our wonderful
young grandchildren.
I pray that you will be blessed with a strong faith in Jesus
and that you may live a joyful Christian life!

1. Can I Lose My Salvation?

"Don't forget: Jesus already paid for your ticket!"

(Angelica to her father when he was gravely ill.)

Introduction

One of the saddest things I ever had to do was take one of our seminary students to the Psychiatric Hospital in Chile. This young man had lost touch with reality and was threatening to hurt the secretary and the students. We had to get professional help.

When the head psychiatrist invited me in for an interview about our student, he told me that many of his patients were evangelicals! I was surprised and asked him why he thought that was the case. He answered that it was because of an overwhelming sense of *guilt*. He had nothing against Christianity, but he complained that many churches only emphasize strict rules and negative things, without talking about the love of God and positive things. This often leads to a heavy burden of guilt, leaving them unable to relate to the world in a healthy way.

I don't think this totally explains the problem of our student, but it made me think seriously about what we are teaching in our churches. His comment grieved me deeply, because it should be precisely our relationship with Christ that *frees* us from our guilt and enables us to live joyfully in the world around us. I tell this story so that we can examine ourselves.

Don't get me wrong; the gospel also includes an explanation of sin, the Fall and its consequences, and a warning about judgment. To understand what Christ did for us, we also have to acknowledge our problem of sin. Also, there is a sense of guilt when we have sinned that is legitimate. However, we shouldn't preach these aspects without also highlighting the wonderful message of salvation: the work of Christ, forgiveness, a new life in Christ, and eternal life, all by grace, and not by merit. I have heard many "evangelical" sermons that have nothing of the gospel. They only point to sin and leave the listeners feeling guilty.

I believe that many Christians have not really understood the wonderful implications of the fact that our salvation is completely by grace through faith and that God will never let us go. We can easily fall into a legalistic pattern that keeps us from the joy we could have in Christ.

It can be terrifying to question your salvation or wonder whether you might *lose* your salvation. The purpose of this chapter is to help you find greater peace, freedom from guilt, and certainty of your salvation.

But before answering the question about whether a Christian can lose his salvation, we need to take a closer look at how we *obtain* salvation in the first place. Is it really by faith alone? If so, what place do good works have? Once we receive our salvation, do we need to continue by our own efforts?

A. Romans 1:17

Martin Luther struggled with a sense of guilt, trying to gain his own sanctification through suffering. While in the monastery, he slept on the floor, fasted, and even whipped himself, in a vain attempt to somehow expiate his own sin. He finally found the answer in Romans 1:17.

The reformers highlighted the doctrine of "justification by faith," which is taught in this verse. However, there is a second aspect to this verse which has not received so much attention until recent years: the concept of *sanctification by faith*. There are differing translations of Romans 1:17:

English Standard: "For in it the righteousness of God is revealed from faith for faith, as it is written, 'The righteous shall live by faith.'"

King James: "For therein is the righteousness of God revealed from faith to faith: as it is written, 'The just shall live by faith.'"

New International Version: "For in the gospel a righteousness from God is revealed, a righteousness that is by faith from first to last, just as it is written: 'The righteous will live by faith.'"

In Greek, it says that righteous comes from God *ek pisteos eis pistin,* literally "out of faith into faith." The word *ek* is a preposition often used to describe movement out of something, such as going "out of" the house. The term *eis* is a preposition used to describe movement into something, such as going "into" the house. The idea is that righteousness starts by faith and ends in faith. Although it is somewhat paraphrased, I believe the NIV communicates the concept properly, that righteousness is by faith "from first to last."

This verse is an introduction to the whole letter to the Romans, which deals first with justification (chapters 1-5), then with sanctification (chapters 6-8). What Paul wants to clarify is that our righteousness does not come from ourselves, but from God, and that this righteousness includes both our justification and our sanctification. It is by faith from beginning to end. Many people understand that they are justified by faith, while being confused about their sanctification. They tend to fall into a practical legalism, thinking that they continue their Christian life in their own strength. Their life reflects it by a lack of joy and freedom.

If we compare the Christian life again to taking a trip on a train, the whole trip is made by faith. Underneath the tracks, the ground on which everything stands, is the infinite grace of God.

I have always enjoyed Woody Guthrie's folk song, "This Train is Bound for Glory," but for many years, I didn't think much about the words. Now I wonder if it doesn't communicate the wrong message. "This train don't carry no gamblers, ...no liars, ...no smokers, ...no thieves,..." It only carries "the righteous and the holy." I'm not sure what the composer meant, but if it means you have to be holy to be saved, nobody could get on the train! But if we interpret it in the light of the gospel, remembering that in Christ, we are made righteous and holy, then it means only those who have trusted Him for forgiveness and for help with their sin can ride the train that is bound for glory.

When my father-in-law was sick and aware that he didn't have much time left, he told us he "had his bags packed." I told him I didn't think he needed to take anything, and Angelica said, "Don't forget that Jesus already paid for your ticket."

For Review:

What does Romans 1:17 teach us about salvation? How can we be considered righteous in God's sight?

B. Justified by Faith

Justification has to do with our *legal* relationship with God. It has two aspects: our forgiveness, and our positive righteousness. Because of the death of Christ on the cross, we are forgiven and we are considered righteous. We are not only freed from guilt, but we have the very righteousness of Christ put on our account. The result is that we are delivered from the punishment we deserve.

It's as if we had a book of life which recorded all our thoughts, words, and deeds. Obviously, it would contain many negative annotations. Jesus exchanges our book with all the negative notations for a new one which contains the record of all *His* perfect thoughts, words and deeds. Justification is a divine verdict by which God declares us righteous.

> Romans 3:20-22, 28
> For by works of the law no human being will be justified in his sight, since through the law comes knowledge of sin. But now the righteousness of God has been manifested apart from the law, although the Law and the Prophets bear witness to it— the righteousness of God through faith in Jesus Christ for all who believe. ...For we hold that one is justified by faith apart from works of the law.

If we tried to justify ourselves by our own deeds, it would not be grace. Also, we would have to be absolutely, totally perfect, because God is a holy God, and must punish sin. It would be like trying to jump to the moon. We can't get to the moon without a rocket, and Christ is our "rocket."

Before his conversion, the famous preacher Charles Spurgeon desperately went from church to church. He was hoping to hear somebody explain some special thing he should do to find peace with God. One day when it was snowing heavily, he couldn't go to the church he had planned to attend, so he went to a small chapel close by. He entered quietly and sat at the back. Because of the bad weather, the pastor had not come, and an elder with little education was preaching. The humble man didn't know how to develop a full sermon, and was simply speaking about Jesus on the cross, describing His blood, the nails, and His pain. When he saw the unknown visitor, the preacher pointed his finger at him and said, "Young man, look at Jesus!" From that moment on, Spurgeon's thoughts were fixed on Jesus, imagining Him on the cross dying for him, and he found the peace he had been seeking. He realized that there was nothing more for him to do. This is justification by faith: realizing that Jesus has already taken care of our sin. As my mother-in-law said when she read Romans 8, "If Jesus died for me, what is my problem?" Justification happens only once, when we accept Jesus as our personal Lord and Savior, and we never lose it.

For Review

1. Define justification.

2. Justification has to do with what kind of relationship with God?

3. Note the two aspects of justification.

4. How do we receive justification?

C. Sanctified by Faith

Sanctification has to do with the process of growth and with our personal relationship with Christ. Just as in a marriage, there is a legal relationship and a personal relationship, so it is with God. In a marriage, two people make public promises and sign papers making a legally binding mutual promise. This is over briefly, and they are declared husband and wife. This first legal aspect corresponds to our justification.

But the couple begins to live together, experiencing growth in their relationship. They learn how each other thinks and feels, and how to show love to one another. This second aspect is like our sanctification.

Some people have not realized the full implications of the fact that our sanctification is also a dimension of our *salvation*. It is not something we can obtain by our own efforts, without the supernatural work of the Holy Spirit. Christ saves us from the *guilt* of our sin in justification, and He saves us from the *power* of sin in sanctification.

Romans 6:14
For sin will have no dominion over you, since you are not under law but under grace.

2 Corinthians 5:17
Therefore, if anyone is in Christ, he is a new creation. The old has passed away; behold, the new has come.

Sometimes people begin their Christian life fully trusting Christ for their forgiveness, then soon fall into the muddy swamp of trying to sanctify themselves by their own strength. People may think, "Jesus has given me eternal life, but now I have to work hard to live a holy life here on earth." Others may believe, "I need to be holy so that God will hear my prayers," or "I should strive to attain a high level of spiritual maturity so He can use me to minister to others." It's good to desire to please God with our lives, but often we turn our attention away from the Lord in the process.

This is exactly what happened with the Galatians. They began well, but soon became legalistic, saying that it was necessary to be circumcised and follow the Jewish customs to be saved. I believe that we are doing something similar when we pretend to "earn points" with God or accomplish our own sanctification.

Galatians 3:3
Are you so foolish? Having begun by the Spirit, are you now being perfected by the flesh?

Think about a vine branch that is not connected to the trunk of the plant. Suppose it tries to produce fruit. It simply can't do it! It must be grafted into the vine first. It is just as impossible for a person to sanctify himself by his own efforts.

John 15:4, 5
Abide in me, and I in you. As the branch cannot bear fruit by itself, unless it abides in the vine, neither can you, unless you abide in me. I am the vine; you are the branches. Whoever abides in me and I in him, he it is that bears much fruit, for apart from me you can do nothing.

Going back to the illustration of the trip to the moon, this error would be like getting in a spaceship (justification; he is already saved when he believes) to go to the moon (the culmination of our salvation: eternal life in the presence of God), then while he is part way to the moon flying in space (the process of sanctification), he gets out of the space ship, thinking he can make it just fine by himself the rest of the way!

I remember a young man who called me on the phone saying he couldn't go to work the next day because the bus went too fast. I asked him if it was dangerous, and he said, "No, but the bus driver is sinning by breaking the speed limit." I asked if he had talked with the driver, and he answered, "Yes, but he won't listen to me." I explained that since he had tried to convince him to slow down, and since the bus wasn't really going fast enough to be dangerous, I thought he had done his part, that he was not guilty, and that he should go to work. However, I couldn't convince him to take the bus again, and for a while, he was taking a taxi to work every day.

Several days later, he called me again saying he couldn't go to work for another reason: the people in his office were listening to music that "wasn't edifying." I asked if he had talked to them about it, and again he replied, "Yes, but they don't listen to me." I insisted that there was nothing else he could do, and that it would be better to go to work anyway.

Finally, he stopped working for good, and at the age of thirty years, he was staying home being cared for by his mother. When I went to talk to him, he said he couldn't go outside because "there were too many temptations out there."

Obviously, he had some psychological problems, but he was also profoundly confused about sanctification. He was trying to avoid temptation completely and attempting to control his environment so that he would not commit any sin. What was the result? He ended up sinning anyway, and probably worse still, because he had become totally dependent and irresponsible, making his mother take care of him. Instead of fulfilling the positive commands about what he should do, like loving people, he was only concerned about what he should *not* do. How could he really love anybody this way? This is not the lifestyle that the Lord wants for us! He wants us to be free from guilt and to be trusting Him for our sanctification.

For Review:

1. Define sanctification.

2. Sanctification is about what kind of relationship with God?

3. Why is it important to recognize that sanctification is a dimension of our *salvation*?

4. Why is it important to recognize that sanctification is *by faith*?

D. The Relation Between Faith and Good Works

Where do good works fit in with the concept of salvation by faith alone? Some passages like James 2 and Matthew 25 could give the impression that we are not saved by faith alone, but by faith and works. James 2:26 says, "For as the body apart from the spirit is dead, so also faith apart from works is dead." Matthew 25 teaches that, on judgment day, people will be divided according to those who have done good deeds and those who haven't. How do we explain these passages, in the light of what we have already seen about salvation by faith alone?

The best way to answer this question is to look again at the divine illustration that Jesus himself taught in John 15:

John 15:1-8

I am the true vine, and my Father is the gardener. He cuts off every branch in me that bears no fruit, while every branch that does bear fruit he prunes so that it will be even more fruitful. You are already clean because of the word I have spoken to you. Remain in me, and I will remain in you. No branch can bear fruit by itself; it must remain in the vine. Neither can you bear fruit unless you remain in me.

I am the vine; you are the branches. If a man remains in me and I in him, he will bear much fruit; apart from me you can do nothing. If anyone does not remain in me, he is like a branch that is thrown away and withers; such branches are picked up, thrown into the fire and burned. If you remain in me and my words remain in you, ask whatever you wish, and it will be given you. This is to my Father's glory, that you bear much fruit, showing yourselves to be my disciples.

Jesus gives us an important analogy: He says He is the vine and we are the branches. Then He tells us how to bear fruit: by "remaining in Him." In fact, He makes the point stronger: we *cannot* bear fruit without Him. Finally, He warns that he who does not remain in Him will be thrown into the fire and burned.

If we relate this to the whole question of faith and works, it becomes clear. We are all born as sinners. We are like a branch disconnected from the vine. Then we are told that if we do not bear fruit, we will be condemned. So what can we do?

Can you imagine a loose branch trying to bear grapes to avoid being cast into the fire? For all its effort to push and squeeze, it can't produce fruit! So what can it do? There is only one way of salvation, to be grafted into the vine! How can we be grafted into the vine? By faith!

Once it becomes part of the vine, the branch receives water and minerals, giving it life and enabling it to bear fruit. This is an analogy of faith. By faith we are grafted into the vine and bear fruit.

How do we know if a branch is really connected to the vine? By the grapes! In the life of a Christian, the fruit is evidence of true faith. If there is no fruit, it shows there is no true faith. This is why Jesus can look at a person's good deeds on judgment day to see if there was true faith. The good deeds are not the *cause* of his salvation, but the *evidence* of his faith.

The fatal mistake is to turn these things around. Some people think that they can be saved by producing good works. But this is just like a loose branch trying to produce grapes. They can't do it! They need to first put their faith in Christ, ask Him for forgiveness, turn their hearts and lives over to Him, and ask Him to produce the good works in them. The *Westminster Confession of Faith* says:

> We cannot by our best works merit pardon of sin, or eternal life at the hand of God, by reason of the great disproportion that is between them and the glory to come; and the infinite distance that is between us and God,... (Chapter 16, section 5)

Think about another illustration, an adaptation of Jesus' analogy. Let's suppose that all of us were born as *orange* trees, and that the only trees that can be saved are *apple* trees. On judgment day, God will look at the fruit to see what kind of tree we are. If we have apples, He will let us enter His presence. If we have oranges, we will be separated from Him. What can we do? Start producing apples to make Him think that we are apple trees? No, we can't! The only hope is to be *transformed miraculously* into real apple trees so that the fruit is genuine.

22

This can only happen by faith in Jesus. He gives us new life so that we can bear genuine fruit.

Finally, one more illustration. Think about a traditional light bulb with a filament. What makes it give out light? Is it the light bulb itself that causes light? No, it's the electricity. The light bulb is an instrument, but the electricity is the power. However, if the filament is burned out or broken, the light bulb will not produce light. Think of how this is an analogy of the Christian. We don't cause good deeds; the Holy Spirit does. However, if we do not have faith, there will be no good deeds. Thus the lack of a changed life indicates a lack of true faith.

For Review:

1. What does John 15 teach us about the relationship between faith and good works?

2. Explain the analogies of the trees and the light bulb to illustrate the relation between faith and good works.

E. Passages That Seem to Teach Salvation Can Be Lost

Now after establishing the fact that our Christian life is by faith, from beginning to end, and the fact that good works are evidence of true faith, but not the cause of our salvation, let's consider the main question we want to address in this chapter: *Can I lose my salvation?*

The biblical answer is NO. When you trust the Good Shepherd for your salvation, He takes you into His arms and will never let you go. Nevertheless, some Christians live their whole life terrified that they might eventually lose their salvation and be eternally condemned. I know of people who have gone forward to receive Christ over and over in evangelistic crusades, because they thought they had lost their salvation. This is not the joyful life that the Lord wants us to have.

Before looking at passages to confirm that salvation cannot be lost, let's take a quick look at other passages that need explanation because, at first sight, they might make you think that a believer can lose his or her salvation.

Hebrews 6:4-6
For it is impossible, in the case of those who have once been enlightened, who have tasted the heavenly gift, and have shared in the Holy Spirit, and have tasted the goodness of the word of God and the powers of the age to come, and then have fallen away, to restore them again to repentance, since they are crucifying once again the Son of God to their own harm and holding him up to contempt.

Galatians 5:4
You are severed from Christ, you who would be justified by the law; you have fallen away from grace.

1 Corinthians 10:12
Therefore let anyone who thinks that he stands take heed lest he fall.

What can we say about these texts? First, some people who seem to have "lost their faith" were never really converted. They were "illuminated" and received certain benefits of the Holy Spirit, especially fellowship with believers and other means of grace found in the church: prayer, the Word, and the sacraments. They claimed to be Christians, but they were never born again. This explains Hebrews 6:4-6.

Secondly, some people are really converted, but fall away from the Lord for a time. They may be tangled up in sin and out of fellowship with Christ, but they will return, like the prodigal son (Luke 15:11-32). Or they may be confused about important doctrines, but will later have things clarified. This seems to fit the case of the Galatians in the passage quoted above. The false teachers had led them into legalism. They had been distracted from grace and had taken their eyes off Jesus. But this doesn't mean that they had lost their salvation. Notice that Paul is still confident that they will come to their senses (Galatians 5:10.) Notice also that the Greek word translated "severed" in Galatians 5:4 (καταργέω, katargéo) can also mean something less drastic and less final, such as "to render idle, unemployed, inactivate, inoperative".[2] For example the *New King James* translation says, "You have become estranged from Christ."

Finally, to "fall" or "fall away from grace" could also refer to a temporary situation. Just because someone falls down, it doesn't mean he can never stand up again. This explains both Galatians 5:4 and 1 Corinthians 10:12.

How can we know if a person never was truly saved or is just temporarily out of fellowship with Christ? We can't really be sure. Only God knows.

---

[2] E4's Greek Lexicon (2001). In Greek Dictionary (electronic ed., p. 2). Ephesians Four Group. Logos Research Systems, Inc.

For Review:

What are some of the explanations of passages that might make us think that salvation can be lost?

F. Passages That Teach Salvation Is Never Lost

Since God takes the initiative in our salvation, we can be sure that a true believer never loses it. That is, our eternal life depends on Him, not on ourselves. God is like a father who carries his child across the street in his arms; He will never let him out of his grasp. Let's look at some Bible passages.

As Jesus always taught with concrete illustrations, He emphasized the security of salvation with the analogy of a flock of sheep.

John 10:27-29
My sheep hear my voice, and I know them, and they follow me. I give them eternal life, and they will never perish, and no one will snatch them out of my hand. My Father, who has given them to me, is greater than all, and no one is able to snatch them out of the Father's hand.

Paul, on the other hand, uses more abstract terms and concepts, but nevertheless writes with passion.

Romans 8:38-39
For I am sure that neither death nor life, nor angels nor rulers, nor things present nor things to come, nor powers, nor height nor depth, nor anything else in all creation, will

be able to separate us from the love of God in Christ Jesus our Lord.

Philippians 1:6
...And I am sure of this, that he who began a good work in you will bring it to completion at the day of Jesus Christ.

Read Romans 8:28-30 slowly and thoughtfully. These verses have been called the "unbreakable chain," because they describe some of the stages of salvation, and each stage is inseparably linked to the other. The same people that God knew and predestined are also called, justified and glorified. This means that salvation will not be lost. What God has predestined is certain!

Romans 8:28-30
And we know that for those who love God all things work together for good, for those who are called according to his purpose. For those whom he foreknew he also predestined to be conformed to the image of his Son, in order that he might be the firstborn among many brothers. And those whom he predestined he also called, and those whom he called he also justified, and those whom he justified he also glorified.

To be "foreknown" means that God loved us even before we were born. To be "predestined" to be like Jesus means that God planned in an unchangeable way, not that we would become divine, but that we would become morally like Him. To be "called" means to hear the gospel and become convinced that it is true. There is an "outward" call, in which we hear the gospel, and an "inward" call, in which we are born again and enabled to respond in faith. Both are brought about by the Holy

Spirit working in our hearts. To be "justified" means we are declared righteous. We are forgiven for our sins and we receive Jesus' righteousness on our account. To be "glorified" means to become holy, morally mature like Jesus, which will be the completion of God's purpose for us. Notice that this is linguistically expressed in the past tense, showing that it is a certain promise.

For Review:

Write down all of the aspects of salvation mentioned in Romans 8:28-30. Put them in the same order as they are found in the passage and give a brief description of each.

The fact that salvation cannot be lost doesn't mean the believer can simply become passive and indifferent about his spiritual life. If we are really saved, we will want to please God and we will use the means He has given us to grow spiritually. If someone doesn't even care about living according to God's will, it's a sign that he probably was never converted.

It's important to add that sometimes a truly born-again Christian might doubt his own salvation. It shouldn't happen, but it can happen. Temporarily doubting his own salvation doesn't necessarily mean that he isn't saved.

The solution to this is simply to reclaim the promises of the gospel and the promises cited above about the permanence of salvation. It doesn't help to look at yourself or examine your own life to confirm your salvation. This can lead you to doubt even more. Instead of looking at yourself, look at Christ.

For Personal Application

a) Bible Study

We recommend that you purchase a notebook to keep notes on your reflections and things you are learning from Scripture. You might also write down prayer requests and motives for thanksgiving. This notebook becomes your spiritual diary.

Three simple steps for analyzing a biblical passage are:

(1) Observation: What exactly does the passage *say*? Write down important information.

(2) Interpretation: What does the passage *mean*? Write down your questions about the passage and look for the answers.

(3) Application: Why is it *important*? What does it teach me about God, about myself, about Christ and salvation? How

should my life change in response to this passage? Write down any new truths, examples, or ethical principles.

For this chapter, study Romans 8:28-39. Write in your notebook the phrases and concepts that confirm the fact that salvation is not lost. Think of the importance of this for your own life. Write down your ideas.

b) Prayer

Use Psalm 23 to guide your prayer time.

c) Memorization of Scripture

Romans 1:17
For in the gospel a righteousness from God is revealed, a righteousness that is by faith from first to last, just as it is written: "The righteous will live by faith." (NIV)

John 10:27-29
My sheep hear my voice, and I know them, and they follow me. I give them eternal life, and they will never perish, and no one will snatch them out of my hand. My Father, who has given them to me, is greater than all, and no one is able to snatch them out of the Father's hand. (ESV)

For Further Reflection and Discussion:

1. Have you sometimes struggled with legalism? Have you ever forgotten that sanctification is also by grace through faith? How did this tendency manifest itself? How did it affect you? Were you able to get out of this trap? Or at least begin to? How?

2. Did you ever struggle with libertinism? What helped you get out of that trap?

3. Do you find the explanation of the relationship between faith and good works in this chapter helpful? Do you still have doubts?

4. Are you convinced that a true Christian will never lose his salvation? If so, how does that make you feel? If not, why not?

2. How Can I Have the Fullness of the Spirit?

"They live in the flesh,
but they are not governed by the desires of the flesh.

They pass their days upon earth,
but they are citizens of heaven."

(From an anonymous letter to Diognetus,
possibly from the second century)

What is the "fullness" of the Spirit?
Do all Christians experience it?
Are there two levels of spirituality?

Introduction

I remember the first time I was told I needed to be "baptized" by the Holy Spirit. While I was a student in seminary, I was attending a Bible conference, and my roommate for the weekend asked if I had experienced this blessing. He opened his Bible and showed me passages in Acts, chapters 8 and 19, where people were apparently already believers, but later gained a new relationship with the Spirit and immediately experienced extraordinary manifestations of His power, such as speaking in tongues.

I have to admit that the passages he showed me began to create doubts in my mind. Maybe there was a second level of spirituality that I hadn't experienced.

A few years later, during my first years in the ministry, I visited a charismatic church to see what it was like. Some friends of mine, new Christians, had been attending this church on Wednesday evenings, and they were excited about their wonderful experiences. They seemed full of joy, so I was curious to see what was happening in those services. The service itself was uplifting. The sermon about "resting in Christ" was biblical, Christ-centered, practical, and it kept my attention the whole hour. Afterwards, they invited people who wanted to speak in tongues to stay afterwards and meet in one of the back rooms. Again, out of curiosity, I decided to see what it was like.

I asked the pastor if I could just sit in the back and listen, and he said sure. There were about 15 people who came. He began by reading John 20:22: "And when he had said this, he breathed on them and said to them, 'Receive the Holy Spirit.'" He pointed out that the disciples received the Holy Spirit at this point, right? Then he continued with Acts 2:4: "And they were all filled with the Holy Spirit and began to speak in other tongues as the Spirit gave them utterance." He argued that after receiving the Spirit, the disciples experienced a "filling" of the Spirit at Pentecost and consequently spoke in tongues.

He told the group that they already had the Spirit if they believed in Jesus, but that they had not been "filled" with the Spirit. Once they were "filled," they would speak in tongues. He proceeded to pray for them and then told them to repeat after him. He began to whisper the phrase, "Thank you, Jesus!" over and over again, faster and faster, until the whole group, except for one girl, was mumbling unintelligible syllables, excited that they were now "speaking in tongues." The girl began to sob, obviously disappointed. It seemed forced and false to me, but it began to stir up questions again.

Finally, after a few more years, as a missionary in Chile, while teaching classes in our seminary, I had another experience that caused concern. Some of our students were visiting charismatic churches and stirring up the desire among the students to speak in tongues. It seemed positive in some ways, because they really seemed excited about their relationship with the Lord. Nevertheless, I wasn't comfortable with the division that I saw them making, as if to say: Some of you Christians just "have" the Holy Spirit, but we have been "filled" or "baptized" with the Spirit.

I began to take a closer look at the Book of Acts and some of Paul's teachings on the Holy Spirit. I also read books on the topic, by authors from differing perspectives. I found some passages difficult to understand initially. Acts 8:4-24 seems to describe some believers in Samaria who had not yet received the Holy Spirit. Acts 19:1-6 also seems to indicate that there were believers in Ephesus who had not received the Holy Spirit. When Paul asked them about it, they said they hadn't ever heard of the Holy Spirit (v. 2)!

There are many questions regarding the work and gifts of the Holy Spirit that have caused debate. However, in this chapter, I want to focus especially on the meaning of the fullness of the Spirit and on the question of whether there are two levels of spirituality.

For Review:

1. Describe some of the issues that cause confusion regarding the work of the Holy Spirit.

2. What are the main questions to be studied in this chapter?

A. General Observations from Paul's Epistles

A principle of Bible interpretation is that we should give priority to didactic passages for establishing doctrines. Historical passages can teach us many things, but they are not necessarily normative. For example, the fact that Paul supported himself by making tents doesn't become a commandment for all missionaries to do the same. When we consider doctrinal issues or ethical issues, we should look first at the portions of Scripture that had the purpose of teaching about those subjects. Therefore, let's look at some passages in Paul's teaching epistles to see if they help us interpret the events narrated in Acts. According to Paul's didactic passages:

1. Every Christian has the Holy Spirit.

One very important point was confirmed as I began my studies: every Christian has the Holy Spirit. Paul makes it clear in his letter to the Romans and in his first letter to the Corinthians.

Romans 8:9
...And if anyone does not have the Spirit of Christ, he does not belong to Christ.

1 Corinthians 12:13
For we were all baptized by one Spirit into one body-- whether Jews or Greeks, slave or free--and we were all given the one Spirit to drink.

The Holy Spirit is the spirit of Jesus, and if anyone has Christ, he has the Spirit. It is the Holy Spirit that converts us, that unites us, and that guides us. It is a contradiction in terms to think of a Christian who does not have the Holy Spirit. The blessing of having the Spirit does not depend on any special experience after conversion; all believers already have it.

2. Every Christian has gifts of the Holy Spirit to benefit the Church.

1 Corinthians 12 is key to understanding the operation of the Holy Spirit. Paul indicates that each Christian has some spiritual gift, some manifestation of the Spirit for the edification of the church:

1 Corinthians 12:7
To each is given the manifestation of the Spirit for the common good.

3. Not all Christians have the same gifts.

However, there is diversity of gifts among Christians. Paul says, "Now there are varieties of gifts, but the same Spirit." (1 Corinthians 12:4) Just like the human body has different parts, so does Christ's Body, the Church. For example, not all are apostles or prophets or teachers. Not all speak in tongues. (1 Corinthians 12:11-19).

4. Spiritual gifts are not necessarily a sign of maturity.

There were many manifestations of extraordinary gifts in the church at Corinth, but the church was not mature.

1 Corinthians 3:1
But I, brothers, could not address you as spiritual people, but as people of the flesh, as infants in Christ.

We shouldn't measure other people's spirituality by the gifts they have received or the experiences they have had.

5. The Spirit helps all Christians become more like Christ.

Paul encourages us to "walk by the Spirit," to be "led by the Spirit," to "live by the Spirit," and to "keep in step with the Spirit" (Galatians 5:16, 16, 25). This allows us to defeat the "works of the flesh" and live a life that is more like Christ. In addition to the *gifts* of the Spirit, all Christians have the *fruit* of the Spirit available to us. This fruit is not produced by our own efforts and it doesn't come quickly. It is a new lifestyle that the Holy Spirit develops in us.

Galatians 5:22-23
But the fruit of the Spirit is love, joy, peace, patience, kindness, goodness, faithfulness, gentleness, self-control; against such things there is no law.

For Review:

1. What general observations about the Holy Spirit taken from Paul's epistles are mentioned in this section?

2. Why are spiritual gifts given to us?

3. Mention the different aspects of the fruit of the Spirit.

B. The Terms in Acts are Interchangeable.

Some people, like the pastor of the church I mentioned above, make distinctions between phrases such as "receiving" the Holy Spirit and being "filled" or "baptized" by the Spirit. I went through different passages, especially in the Book of Acts, to see if different terms were used to make intentional distinctions. I found that the phrases are interchangeable and don't justify making technical distinctions. Consider the terms used in the following passages:

Acts 1:5-8 and 2:4-18 (Jerusalem on the Day of Pentecost). These verses use four different phrases to describe the same event on the day of Pentecost: you will be "baptized" by the Holy Spirit (1:5), you will receive power when the Holy Spirit has "come upon you" (1:8), they were all "filled" with the Holy Spirit

(2:4), and this fulfills the prophecy of Joel that says God would "pour out" His Spirit on them (2:17,18).

Acts 8:14-18 (Samaria). In this passage, three different phrases are used to describe the same experience in Samaria. First, Peter and John prayed that they might "receive" the Holy Spirit, because He had not yet "fallen on" any of them (v. 16). Then they "received" the Holy Spirit (v. 17), and Simon sees that the Spirit was "given" to them (v. 18). Notice that these were people who had believed the good news and had experienced the sacrament of baptism (v. 12).

Acts 10:44-47 and 11:15-16 (Caesarea). In chapter 10, several different phrases are used to describe the experience of the centurion Cornelius and his family in Caesarea: the Holy Spirit "fell on" everyone (10:44), the gift of the Holy Spirit was "poured out" on them (10:45), and Peter said that they had "received" the Holy Spirit (10:47). In chapter 11, Peter gives a report in Jerusalem about what happened to Cornelius and his family. He says the Spirit "fell on them" (v. 15) and that this fulfilled the promise in Joel about being "baptized" with the Holy Spirit (v. 16).

Considering the use of terminology in these passages, it's obvious that they are interchangeable. We can't make technical and theological distinctions simply on the basis of these terms. It doesn't allow for telling somebody they have already "received" the Spirit but they have not been "baptized" by the Spirit, or that they have been "baptized" by the Spirit but they have not been "filled" with the Spirit. There is no evidence that supports the concept of two levels of spirituality.

For Review:

1. What are the observations about some of the terms regarding experiences with the Holy Spirit in the Book of Acts?

2. Do these observations reveal a distinction between two levels of spirituality?

C. "Full" of the Spirit and "Filled" with the Spirit

While I couldn't agree with the technical distinctions some people make in the terminology used in Acts, as I was studying these passages in the Greek version, I did come across a helpful grammatical distinction. I saw a distinction between being "full" of the Spirit and being "filled" with the Spirit. These are two different linguistic forms: an adjective and a verb.

1. Being "full" of the Spirit

Sometimes Luke uses the *adjective*, "full" (often πλήρεις, *pleres,* in Greek), to describe a *characteristic* of a person. We might use an adjective to say a person is "strong" or "pretty," for example. A person who is "full" of the Spirit is spiritually mature and shows the fruit of the Spirit. This adjective form is used to speak of the deacons and of Barnabas.

Acts 6:3
Therefore, brothers, pick out from among you seven men of good repute, *full* (πλήρεις, plereis) of the Spirit and of wisdom, whom we will appoint to this duty.

Acts 11:24
For he was a good man, *full* (πλήρης, pleres) of the Holy
Spirit and of faith...

We all probably know people who seem "full" of the Spirit.
They may be very loving, very joyful, or show the fruit of the
spirit in some special way. One of my professors at seminary
always seemed to have a close relationship with the Lord. If you
spoke to him about any problem, he would stop what he was
doing and pray for you, wherever you were at the time. To me,
he was a person "full of the Spirit."

2. Being "filled" with the Spirit

In other cases, Luke uses a *verb* form in passive voice
(usually the verb πίμπλημι, *pímplemi,* in Greek), to describe an
experience of being "filled" with the Spirit in preparation for
some ministry. The passive voice of a verb is used to show that
the subject received the action, for example that a book was
"bought," or a house was "painted." In this case, a person was
"filled" with the Holy Spirit.

This verb form is used to describe what happened at
Pentecost and what happened to Peter and Paul on different
occasions.

Acts 2:4
And they were all *filled* (ἐπλήσθησαν, from pímplemi) with
the Holy Spirit and began to speak in other tongues as the
Spirit gave them utterance.

Acts 4:8
Then Peter, *filled* with the Holy Spirit, said to them, "Rulers
of the people and elders..."

Acts 13:9-10

But Saul, who was also called Paul, filled with the Holy Spirit, looked intently at him and said, "You son of the devil,..."

See also Acts 4:31 and Acts 9:17. Luke uses similar *verb* forms also in his gospel to describe the experiences of John the Baptist in his mother's womb (Luke 1:15), Elizabeth (1:41), and Zechariah (1:67). Paul uses a passive verb form in Ephesians 5:18 ("be filled with the Spirit"). In this case the verb is pleróo (πληρόω). There may be exceptions to this pattern, but the distinction is normally clear.

Notice that someone who has been "filled" with the Spirit may later be "filled" again. See the experiences of Peter in Acts 2:1, 4:8 and 4:31. See the repeated cases of Paul in Acts 9:17 and 13:9. The same thing happens to the disciples as a group (see Acts 2:4 and Acts 13:52).

This doesn't mean the person lost the Holy Spirit and needs to receive Him again. It's better to understand these experiences as moments when the Holy Spirit has repeatedly manifested His presence and power in a special way.

You may have been "filled" with the Spirit in occasions to do something special. Maybe you were talking to someone about the gospel and suddenly thoughts and Bible passages came to your mind unexpectedly. Maybe you have felt moved to write to someone to encourage her, only later to find out that she was going through a rough time and needed a kind word. Maybe you were moved to pray for someone, but you weren't sure why. These unusual moments may have been experiences of being filled with the Spirit.

3. Conclusion

The difference between these two expressions is like the difference between saying a person is "strong" and saying a person is "lifted up." In the first case, the word describes the *person*, and in the second case, the phrase describes what *happens* to the person. In the first case, the characteristic is usually more permanent, but in the second case, the experience is temporal.

The result of a person being "filled" with the Spirit is some special ministry. God sovereignly gives this when someone needs it. Often the task is to teach or preach the Word or to prophesy. This can happen to the same person repeatedly. It's something that comes and goes as the Lord provides.

As mentioned previously, having such an experience does not necessarily indicate spiritual maturity (1 Corinthians 3:1) On the other hand, the person who is "full" of the Spirit is considered trustworthy for leadership, because he shows spiritual maturity. Between the two chapters on spiritual gifts (1 Corinthians 12 and 14), Paul inserts a section on love. He insists that the gifts of tongues, prophecy, knowledge or faith, mean nothing without love.

1 Corinthians 13:1
If I speak in the tongues of men and of angels, but have not love, I am a noisy gong or a clanging cymbal.

What we should seek most earnestly is the characteristic of being "full" of the Spirit. We should use the means of grace to grow spiritually: prayer, the Word, the sacraments, and Christian fellowship. Then the Lord will equip us for the tasks that He calls us to do, in His way and at the moment He desires. If we are faithful to Him and watching for the opportunities He gives us to help others, He will "fill" us with the Spirit whenever it is necessary.

When a baby is born, he or she begins to grow immediately, then soon becomes a child, then an adolescent, then an adult. He becomes stronger and stronger as he matures. Along the way, as he grows, he may need special adrenalin for challenging tasks, such as running a race or playing a basketball game.

The same thing happens in our spiritual lives. When we are born again, we already have the Holy Spirit. Then we begin to grow spiritually. The goal is maturity, to be more and more "full" of the Spirit. However, along the way, we do need some special experiences of being "filled" with the Spirit to minister to other people. These experiences are repeated as many times and in as many ways as the Lord desires.

Full and Filled with the Spirit

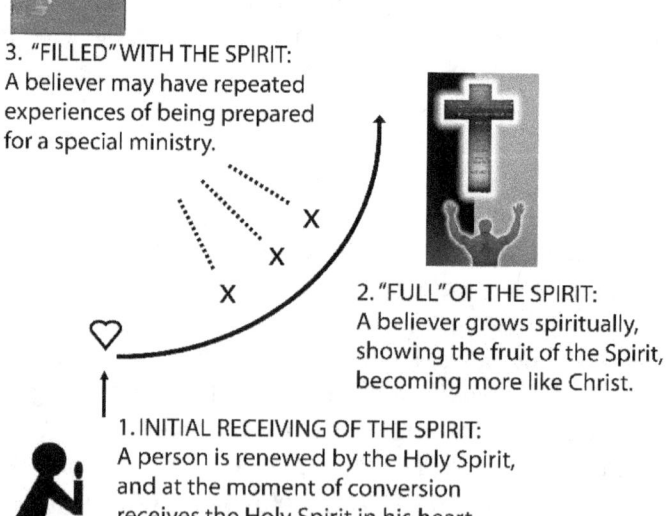

3. "FILLED" WITH THE SPIRIT:
A believer may have repeated experiences of being prepared for a special ministry.

2. "FULL" OF THE SPIRIT:
A believer grows spiritually, showing the fruit of the Spirit, becoming more like Christ.

1. INITIAL RECEIVING OF THE SPIRIT:
A person is renewed by the Holy Spirit, and at the moment of conversion receives the Holy Spirit in his heart for sanctification and guidance.

This scheme does not allow for two levels of spirituality. All believers have the Holy Spirit, then go through a process of growth (the curve), accompanied by possible experiences of being filled for special purposes (the x's).

This helps understand Acts 2 (Jerusalem).

This scheme helps avoid misunderstandings with passages like Acts 2. The disciples were apparently born-again believers by this time. Just exactly when they were converted is not so clear. At least in the case of Peter, it looks like he expressed faith in Jesus before the transfiguration (Matthew 16:13-20). This faith would not be possible without the work of the Holy Spirit in his heart. Then Jesus breathed on the disciples and said, "Receive the Holy Spirit" in John 20:22. Finally, at Pentecost, Peter and the other disciples were "filled with the Spirit" and began to preach in other languages to the crowd in Jerusalem.

We should understand this to mean that the disciples were "filled" with the Spirit for special ministries *both in John 20 and in Acts 2.* When Jesus has them "receive" the Spirit, it doesn't mean that they had not already received the Spirit previously, but that they needed a special work of the Spirit to preach the gospel. Notice that just before Jesus breathed on them to receive the Spirit, He said, "As the Father has sent me, even so I am sending you." (John 20:21) They also needed a special work of the Spirit to preach to the multitude at Pentecost, a key moment in the beginning of the expansion of the church. The miraculous manifestations confirmed the authority of the apostles. The fact that people heard them speak in their own tongues was also a symbol of the inclusion of the Gentiles and of a reversal of the punishment of the Tower of Babel. Instead of setting a new pattern for all Christians in all times, and instead of establishing two levels of spirituality, it is an example of how the Spirit sometimes fills us repeatedly for special ministries.

For Review:

1. Explain the difference between being "full" of the Holy Spirit and being "filled" with the Holy Spirit. What are the results of each?

2. What are the practical implications of the scheme presented in this section?

3. How does this scheme help understand the experiences in Acts 2?

E. Acts Describes a Unique Period of Transition.

I would like to mention some theological points that will also help understand the special period narrated in Acts. Because it was a unique historical moment, a time of transition from the Old Testament to the New Testament, some unusual things happened.

1. The special manifestations in Acts were evidence of the transition to a new age with a new power of the Holy Spirit.

The Holy Spirit came in a new and extraordinary way on the Day of Pentecost, announcing the new era which began when Jesus was exalted at the right hand of the Father in heaven. Peter highlights this fact when he explains what happened at Pentecost.

> Acts 2:33
> Being therefore exalted at the right hand of God, and having received from the Father the promise of the Holy Spirit, he has poured out this that you yourselves are seeing and hearing.

The special experiences narrated in Acts confirm that Jesus has sent the Holy Spirit to work in a new way. He comes to us more permanently, more powerfully, and more intimately. The difference was so great that John had said that the Spirit "had not been given, because Jesus was not yet glorified." (John 7:39)

Apparently, the Pentecost experience didn't happen in other locations exactly at the same moment. There were believers outside of Jerusalem who already had received the Holy Spirit but didn't experience the new power until later. New manifestations of the Pentecost power were taking place in stages, in different times and in different places.

It was as if an empty lake had been filled on the day of Pentecost. As the water rose, it flowed downhill in streams to reach different places later. One of my favorite places in Chile is in the southern Andes mountains near a lake called Caburgua. Streams come from the lake, sometimes flowing underground, that produce beautiful waterfalls, gushing springs, and deep ponds in the region below. We could think of Jerusalem as the higher lake that was filled on the day of Pentecost, then Samaria, Caesarea and Ephesus are like the waterfalls, springs and ponds produced later.

> Jerusalem
>> Samaria
>>> Caesarea
>>>> Ephesus

This helps understand Acts 19:1-7 (Ephesus).

Considering the transition period helps understand the situation in Ephesus recorded in Acts 19. When Paul found some "disciples" at Ephesus, he asked them, "Did you receive the Holy Spirit when you believed?" They answered, "No, we have not even heard that there is a Holy Spirit" (v. 2). The question is, how could these disciples be true believers who hadn't even heard of the Holy Spirit or "received" Him? The answer is found in Paul's question to them about their baptism: "Into what then were you baptized?" They said they had been baptized into John's baptism (vs. 3). Paul explained that "John baptized with the baptism of repentance, telling the people to believe in the one who was to come after him, that is, Jesus" (v. 4).

It's very likely that these "disciples" had received teaching from Apollos before he learned some important things. In the last verses of chapter 18, we read that Apollos had been in Ephesus (Acts 18:24). It says, "He had been instructed in the way of the Lord, and he spoke with great fervor and taught about Jesus accurately, though he knew only of the baptism of John." Priscilla and Aquila invited him to their home and "explained to him the way of God more adequately" (18:25-26).

The best explanation is that the "disciples" in Ephesus were not yet born-again believers and therefore hadn't received the Spirit in any sense of the word. They were probably only followers of John the Baptist. When Paul comes, he baptizes them *in the name of Jesus* and lays hands on them. The Spirit comes upon them and they begin to speak in tongues and prophesy (vv. 6-7). This situation certainly isn't the pattern for all Christians since Pentecost.

2. The special manifestations in Acts were also evidence that the *Gentiles* could be saved, become part of the people of God, and receive the Holy Spirit.

In addition to the new power of the Holy Spirit after Pentecost, there was another important change in the development of God's kingdom: the great inclusion of the Gentiles. It was important to confirm this change with something observable. And one very clear way was to show that the new believers among the Gentiles also had the new power of the Holy Spirit.

God illustrates spiritual truths through important historical events. These events become theological "plays." For example, the exodus shows His power to free His people from slavery, illustrating that salvation is freedom from slavery to sin. The great flood teaches us about judgment and renewal. The exile shows what it means to be separated from God and brought back.

In a similar way, the inclusion of the Gentiles plays out historically the gospel of reconciliation. While the Fall brought conflict into all relationships, salvation in Christ brings reconciliation (Ephesians 1:10), healing the effects of the Fall.

Many miracles and new revelation accompany special events like the flood, the exodus, and the exile. The greatest concentration of miracles and new revelation comes during the central event of history, the coming of Christ. The miracles confirm the truth of the gospel and show the authority of Jesus. Then after Jesus' ascension, there were also many special manifestations among the first Gentiles who believed in Him to show that they also were saved, that they also received the Holy Spirit, and that they also belonged to God's people. At Pentecost, the fact that people from different nations were hearing the gospel in their own language points to the healing of the curse of Babel. Sin confuses and divides; Christ enlightens and unites.

This helps understand Acts 10-11 (Cornelius and the Gentiles at Caesarea).

This emphasis on the inclusion of Gentiles is highlighted in the case of Cornelius, his relatives and his close friends, narrated in Acts 10. Through visions and angels, God arranged for Peter to go explain the gospel to this "upright and God-fearing" man in Caesarea. This was difficult for Peter at first, because, as he said, it was considered "unlawful" to associate with Gentiles. But God had shown him in a vision that he should not call any man "common" or "unclean." (10:28) As he preached about Jesus, they believed, were immediately filled with the Spirit, and began to speak in tongues, praising God.

The gift of tongues was an obvious sign to Peter that the Gentiles at the house of Cornelius had received the Holy Spirit (Acts 10:45-47). He later testified to what he had witnessed to convince others in Jerusalem that the Gentiles were also receiving eternal life.

Acts 11:15–18
"As I began to speak, the Holy Spirit fell on them just as on us at the beginning. ... If then God gave the same gift to them as he gave to us when we believed in the Lord Jesus Christ, who was I that I could stand in God's way?" When they heard these things they fell silent. And they glorified God, saying, "Then to the Gentiles also God has granted repentance that leads to life."

Since they were immediately filled with the Spirit upon believing, there is no theological difficulty. This is obviously not a case where born-again Christians did not receive the Spirit until a later time or a case where Christians had received the Spirit, but later moved up to a higher spiritual level by being "baptized" in the Spirit or "filled" with the Spirit.

It also helps understand Acts 8 (Samaria).

The inclusion of the Gentiles is also a major theme in Acts 8. Simon the sorcerer had been practicing his magic in this city and had many followers. Then Philip went to preach the gospel. He performed signs and miracles, casting out evil spirits and healing the sick. Many who had been following Simon believed Philip and were baptized. In fact, Simon himself "believed and was baptized." (vs. 13) When word of this came to Jerusalem, they sent Peter and John to them.

Acts 8:12-17
But when they believed Philip as he preached good news about the kingdom of God and the name of Jesus Christ, they were baptized, both men and women. Even Simon himself believed, and after being baptized he continued with Philip. And seeing signs and great miracles performed,

he was amazed. Now when the apostles at Jerusalem heard that Samaria had received the word of God, they sent to them Peter and John, who came down and prayed for them that they might receive the Holy Spirit, for he had not yet fallen on any of them, but they had only been baptized in the name of the Lord Jesus. Then they laid their hands on them and they received the Holy Spirit.

At first it appears that the Samaritans believed in Jesus when they heard Philip preach, but did not have the Holy Spirit at all until Peter and John came and prayed for them and laid hands on them. However, because of what we have studied previously, we are encouraged to look for another explanation.

Probably the best explanation is that they were not really converted yet. To be precise, it only says that they had "believed Philip" (v. 8) and that they had "received the Word of God" (v. 14). Sometimes people accept truths of the Word in their heads, without being born again. The case of Simon seems to support this idea. Simon "believed" and was baptized, but he also wanted to *buy* the power of the Holy Spirit! Peter says he is "full of bitterness and captive to sin" (v. 23). He says, "... Your heart is not right with God" (v. 21) and, "May your money perish with you!" (v. 20). This would be very strong language to use with a true believer! It's difficult to believe that Simon was truly converted.

Given the social and religious context, something extraordinary had to happen to show the world that even these Samaritans were true Christians, and that they too had the Holy Spirit. It would also be important for recognized leaders like Peter and John to be witnesses. For centuries, prejudice had divided the Jews from the Samaritans. The Samaritans were a mixed race, despised by the Jews. It must have been hard for other believers, especially among the Jews, to accept the fact that they too were really part of the new People of God. The evidence was that they experienced amazing miracles when they were filled by the Spirit.

For Review:

1. What two extraordinary historical transitions were evidenced by the special manifestations of the Holy Spirit in Acts?

2. Explain how considering these two transitions help interpret the experiences narrated in Acts 8, 10, and 19.

Conclusion

If you are a born-again Christian, you already have the Holy Spirit. You should concern yourself with growing in Christ, becoming more and more "full" of the Spirit. This involves using the means of grace, but above all, it comes from trusting the Spirit to give you greater love, joy, peace, patience, kindness goodness, faithfulness, gentleness and self-control (Galatians 5:22). Remember, this is the fruit of the Spirit, not something you can produce on your own.

The Lord may also give you the blessing of being "filled" with the Spirit for special ministry purposes. The experience of being "filled" with the Spirit is not something you receive once and for all, leaving you on a higher spiritual level. Rather, it is something you can experience repeatedly.

The miraculous manifestations were especially frequent at the time of the New Testament, meant to testify to the new epoch after the victory of Christ and to announce the inclusion of the Gentiles. This doesn't mean that miraculous manifestations ceased after the time of the New Testament, but it does mean that what happened at that time is not necessarily to be expected as the normal experience for all Christians at all times.

The different experiences narrated in Acts suggest that Christians may also have differing experiences today. We shouldn't put pressure on other Christians to have the same experiences we have, and we shouldn't pretend to measure their spiritual maturity by the experiences they have had. Even more importantly, we should avoid any thought of two kinds of Christians or two levels of spirituality. It's sadly ironic that the very portions of Scripture that were meant to show that we are all united in Christ, that we all share the same Spirit, have been used incorrectly to divide us!

The Essential Points

1. Every Christian has the Holy Spirit upon conversion, and every Christian has spiritual gifts.
2. We should concern ourselves especially with growing in the fruit of the Spirit, becoming "full" of the Spirit.
3. We also may be "filled" with the Spirit on special occasions to carry out a special ministry.

For Personal Application

a) Bible Study

Study 1 Corinthians, chapters 12-14. Write down what you learn about spiritual gifts in these chapters.

b) Prayer

Use Galatians 5:22-23 to guide your prayer time. Ask the Lord to give you this fruit of the Spirit, and that He also give this same fruit of the Spirit to your family, your friends, and members of your church.

c) Memorization of Scripture

1 Corinthians 12:7
To each is given the manifestation of the Spirit for the common good. (ESV)

For Further Reflection and Discussion:

1. How has your concept of the work of the Holy Spirit changed after studying this chapter?

2. How can you develop more fruit of the Spirit? In what areas do you think you need to grow most?

3. Have you experienced being "filled" with the Spirit for some ministry? Explain your experience.

3. How Should We Use the O.T. Laws Today?

"Whatever might be the amount of darkness under the law, the fathers were not ignorant of the road in which they ought to walk. Though the law is not equal to the splendor of noon, yet, as it is sufficient to direct a journey, travelers do not wait till the sun is fully risen. Their portion of light resembled the dawn,..."

(John Calvin, Commentary on Galatians 3:23)

Introduction

When I was a boy, I remember a discussion regarding the validity of capital punishment in Sunday School. Someone read Exodus 21:12 to support its practice: "Whoever strikes a man so that he dies shall be put to death." There you are! It couldn't be clearer! All murderers should be put to death! ...Or is it so clear? My doubts arose when I continued reading verse 17 in the same chapter: "Whoever curses his father or his mother shall be put to death." This was shocking! It also confused me that they argued for capital punishment on the basis of verse 12, but they seemed to ignore the application of the same punishment for cursing your parents found in verse 17. This issue continued to puzzle me for many years.

How should we use the Old Testament law today? Some people think these laws have little to teach us today, while others believe that we should practice them exactly like they were supposed to in the Old Testament times. In seminary, one of my classmates, Greg Bahnsen, was defending this second view, and he eventually became a well-known writer on the subject. I have been troubled by interviews on TV with pastors regarding punishments established in the Old Testament for certain sins such as homosexual relations. Often they don't know what to say when the interviewer asks them what they think about it. In this article I hope to help clear up this confusion.

A. Differences Between the O.T. and the N.T.

The question brings up other biblical-theological issues. What changes occurred between the Old Testament and the New Testament in general? Were people saved by works in the Old Testament? What was the purpose of all the ceremonial laws and the ritual sacrifices in the Old Testament? What about the modern nation of Israel? Is it still God's chosen people with a divine right to the same territory, or does the Church replace Israel as the people of God? What about the covenants? Does the *New* Covenant completely replace the *Old* Covenant? The Bible is not a static book of only rules and teachings; it is a dynamic history with stages of development. What are the changes? How do they affect our use of the law today?

First, let's be clear on one important thing: people who lived in Old Testament times were saved in the same way as New Testament people, by faith in Jesus Christ. In the Old Testament they looked forward to the Messiah, and since the New Testament, we look back, knowing that Jesus Christ has already come. In both cases, it is Jesus who saves, and it is faith in Him that enables us to receive eternal life. Even in the Garden of Eden, Adam and Eve heard the promise of the Messiah. Speaking to the serpent, God tells him:

> Genesis 3:15
> I will put enmity between you and the woman, and between your offspring and her offspring; he shall bruise your head, and you shall bruise his heel.

This is considered the first proclamation of the gospel. It's the promise of the victory of God's people over His enemies, the victory of the descendant of Eve over Satan. Even Adam and Eve were expected to put their faith in this promise.

The message of salvation by faith instead of salvation by works should have been clear when God took away the fig leaves that they had used to cover themselves and provided garments of skin (Genesis 1:21). Consider the fact that animals had to be killed to provide these new coverings. This pointed to the sacrifice of Jesus, the offspring of Adam and Eve.

Abraham was justified by his faith, not by his works. (Genesis 15:6: "And he believed the LORD, and he counted it to him as righteousness.") Paul highlights this in Romans, chapter four, using Abraham as an example for us today.

No one has ever been saved by their good works (Romans 3:20: "For by works of the law no human being will be justified in his sight, since through the law comes knowledge of sin."). The Old Testament law was an instrument to show the need for forgiveness and a savior, pointing to Jesus. (Galatians 3:24: "So then, the law was our guardian until Christ came, in order that we might be justified by faith.") The ceremonial system with all the rites and sacrifices points to Jesus, the "lamb of God." There are many symbols of Jesus, such as the rock (See Numbers 20 and 1 Corinthians 10:14), the manna (Exodus 16 and John 6: 25-59), and the bronze serpent lifted up on a pole (Numbers 21 and John 3:14). The prophets, priests and kings, although weak, were figures of Jesus who perfectly fulfilled the roles of prophet, priest and king. Jesus Himself indicated that the whole Old Testament spoke of Him. (Luke 24:27: "And beginning with Moses and all the Prophets, he interpreted to them in all the Scriptures the things concerning himself.")

But not everyone understood this. Paul insists that the error of Israel was precisely in thinking that they could obtain salvation by their own works. (Romans 9:32: "...Because they did not pursue it by faith, but as if it were based on works. ...")

Secondly, within the one plan of salvation, there were *developments*. Theologians speak of the "covenant of grace", which unites the two testaments. The "covenant of grace" is the promise of salvation by faith in Jesus Christ. After the Fall, it has been the only way of salvation. However, there were different ways in which God offered this covenant, modifying its expression for different times under different leaders. For example, the covenant with Abraham focused on the promise of a people and a place (Genesis 17:1-8). The covenant with Moses provided the laws for the nation of Israel, including guidelines for the priests and the worship ceremonies (Exodus 19:3-6). The covenant with David highlighted the promise of a descendant who would rule the kingdom forever (2 Samuel 7:12-17).

Even more important changes were made when Jesus came. In fact, these differences are so important that the author of Hebrews speaks of a "better covenant" (Hebrews 7:22) and a "new covenant" (Hebrews 9:15). The very name "New Testament" is the translation of a phrase in Greek that means "new covenant." Again, this doesn't mean there is a new way of salvation; fundamentally it is the same plan, the same "covenant of grace." Dennis Johnson uses the illustration of one river with different tributaries which empty into the lake of the New Testament.[3]

---

[3] Dennis E. Johnson, *Journeys with Jesus; Every Path in the Bible Leads us to Christ* (Phillipsburg, NJ: P&R Publishing, 2018), p. 44.

THE COVENANT OF GRACE

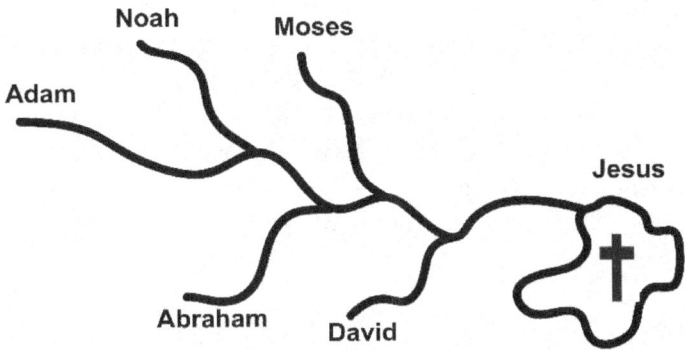

THE OLD TESTAMENT   **THE NEW TESTAMENT**
Covenants with Key Leaders   **The Covenant in Christ**

What are some of these changes under the new covenant? There are huge advantages to living on this side of the cross:

1) We have the law written on our hearts (Hebrews 10:16)
2) We have access to greater power of the Holy Spirit (John 7:37-39).
3) We have already seen the victory over sin and death, won by Jesus (Colossians 2:15).
4) Sin can no longer dominate us (Romans 6:14).

John Calvin points out several differences between the Old and New Covenants: 1. Under the Old Covenant, the blessings were tasted in earthly benefits, whereas under the New Covenant, they are tasted "directly." 2. The Old Covenant was

65

revealed in images and shadows, but the New Covenant in substance. 3. The Old Covenant was "literal," whereas the New Covenant is "spiritual," written on the heart, preaching life and mercy. 4. The Old Covenant was of "bondage," and the New Covenant is of "freedom." 5. The Old Covenant was for one nation, but the New Covenant included the Gentiles. [4]

In conclusion, we shouldn't minimize the contrast between the Old Testament and the New Testament, because the new benefits are amazing. Nor should we exaggerate the changes. We should be especially careful not to assume that there was another plan of salvation during the Old Testament. This would seriously distort the message of the entire Bible.

For Review:

1. What unites the Old Testament and the New Testament?

2. How were people saved in the time of the Old Testament?

3. What are some of the important changes that have occurred under the "new covenant" in the New Testament?

B. Two Extremes

How do these differences help us know how to use the Old Testament law today?

---

[4] John Calvin, *Institutes of the Christian Religion,* ed. John T. McNeill, (Philadelphia: Westminster Press, 1967, Book 2, chapter 11, sections 1-14) 1:449-464.

There are two extreme positions regarding the use of the Old Testament law today. One view says that the Old Testament law was only for the Jews before the time of Christ, and that it is no longer applicable for us since the time of the New Testament. On the other extreme we find the view that all the Old Testament law is applicable for us today, just as it was for the Jews before Christ.

Lewis Sperry Chafer represents the first position. He argued that the Mosaic law was a covenant of works which Israel really should not have accepted at Sinai. They should have appealed to God's grace. The Mosaic law terminated with Christ's death, and we no longer need to keep it.

> It may be concluded then, that the law which was given by Moses was a covenant of works, that it was "added" after centuries of human history, that its reign was terminated by the death of Christ, that it was given to Israel only, and that, since it was never given to Gentiles, the only relation that Gentiles can sustain to it is, without any divine authority, to impose it upon themselves. [5]

Greg Bahnsen represents the second position, sometimes called the "theonomist" view. His key text is Matthew 5:17-18.

Matthew 5:17-18
Do not think that I have come to abolish the Law or the Prophets; I have not come to abolish them but to fulfill them. For truly, I say to you, until heaven and earth pass away, not an iota, not a dot, will pass from the Law until all is accomplished.

---

[5] Lewis Sperry Chafer. *Systematic Theology* 8 vols. (Dallas: Dallas Seminary Press, 1948) 4:166.

He concludes, and this is his main thesis, that,

> Not even the very least extensive number of the very least significant aspect of the Older Testamental law will become invalid until heaven and earth pass away.[6]

The title of his first chapter in the book, *Theonomy in Christian Ethics*, is "The Abiding Validity of the Law in Exhaustive Detail." Bahnsen is especially interested in applying the civil laws of the Old Testament to our governments today.[7]

For Review:

What are the two extreme positions regarding the use of the Old Testament law today?

C. Changes in the Application of the OT Law

These are two extreme positions. I believe the biblical evidence shows that neither of them is correct.

On the one hand, we can't totally disregard the laws of the Old Testament. Jesus leaves no room for that with his comments in Matthew 5:17-18. Neither does Paul. (2 Timothy 3:16: "All Scripture is God-breathed and is useful for teaching, rebuking, correcting and training in righteousness,...")

---

[6] Greg Bahnsen. *Theonomy in Christian Ethics* (Nutley, N.J., Craig Press, 1979), p. 73.

[7] Ibid., pp. 1-3.

On the other hand, Scripture indicates that changes were made in the application of the law under the New Testament. Let's look at a few examples:

1) Forbidden foods. The Lord showed Peter in a vision (Acts 10:9-15) that he could eat many kinds of animals that had been considered "unclean" in the Old Testament period (see Leviticus 11). God tells him, "What God has made clean, do not call common" (Acts 10:15). Paul also expresses this change in Romans 14:1-4.

2) The first council of the New Testament church (Acts 15) met to discuss the issue of keeping the law of Moses. Some Jews insisted that the Gentiles in Antioch should be circumcised and keep the law, but the conclusion of the council was that it wasn't necessary. They asked them to keep some customs in order to avoid conflicts between themselves and the Jews. But they didn't insist that they keep the Law of Moses in the same way as the Old Testament Jews.

In fact, to insist on circumcision became a sign of legalism and a lack of understanding of the gospel. Paul warned the Galatians not to listen to the legalists. (Galatians 5:2: "I, Paul, say to you that if you accept circumcision, Christ will be of no advantage to you.")

3) The observance of the Day of Rest had to be on the Seventh day of the week in the Old Testament. However, Paul indicates that there is now greater freedom regarding how the day is kept. (Romans 14:5: "One person esteems one day as better than another, while another esteems all days alike. Each one should be fully convinced in his own mind." See also Colossians 2:16.)

4) Ordinances for temple worship and ceremonial sacrifices were no longer to be kept after Christ's death and resurrection (Hebrews 10:1-2 says that the sacrifices had "ceased to be offered")

How do we explain these examples? How should we apply the Old Testament law today?

D. Two Important Historical Events

There are two important historical events that help us understand this issue.

1) The first event is that Jesus made the final sacrifice on the cross, putting an end to the sacrificial system. The Old Testament sacrifices were meant to point to Him, and they are no longer necessary.

Hebrews 10:12, 14, 17-18
12) But when Christ had offered for all time a single sacrifice for sins, he sat down at the right hand of God, ...
14) For by a single offering he has perfected for all time those who are being sanctified.
17-18) Then he adds, "I will remember their sins and their lawless deeds no more." Where there is forgiveness of these, there is no longer any offering for sin.

2) The second important event is the inclusion of the Gentiles as part of God's people and the end of the privileged role of the nation of Israel. Before Christ, the nation of Israel was the earthly manifestation of the Kingdom of God. If you wanted to belong to His people, you had to become a citizen of their

nation. However, after Christ, this changed. Now people from different cultures, countries, and languages all around the world are part of His kingdom. Now no political nation is God's special chosen people. No nation represents the Kingdom of God.

Galatians 3:28-29
There is neither Jew nor Greek, slave nor free, male nor female, for you are all one in Christ Jesus. If you belong to Christ, then you are Abraham's seed, and heirs according to the promise.

This is important for our study of the law, because it means that we no longer practice certain aspects of the law that applied to Israel as a nation.

It's also important to keep this in mind as we consider world politics. During the last 2,000 years, Christians all too often have forgotten that God's kingdom is spiritual, not political, and that it now includes believer in all nations from all ethnic groups. Tragically, this has led to many wars, as people attempted to establish God's kingdom by force as a political entity.

For Review:

1. Mention some of the changes made in the New Testament regarding keeping the Old Testament law.

2. What are the two important historical events that help us understand how to use the Old Testament Law today?

E. The Three Aspects of the Law

To understand how to keep the Old Testament law today, it helps to make a distinction between the ceremonial, civil and moral aspects of the law. These aspects of the law are interwoven throughout the Old Testament, like a sweater with three different colors of thread. John Calvin made this distinction in his *Institutes*,[8] and the *Westminster Confession of Faith* teaches the same thing.[9]

a) The ceremonial aspect
This included things like the sacrifices, worship, and customs of purification. We no longer keep this aspect as they did in the Old Testament, because they pointed to Jesus, who ended these ceremonies when He made the last sacrifice on the cross. Nevertheless, we can learn important spiritual truths from these laws and customs.

b) The civil aspect
The purpose of this aspect was to maintain a just treatment among the Jews as a nation. It included the correct use of land and property, as well as punishments for breaking the law. We no longer keep this aspect as in the time of the Old Testament, since the people of God is no longer the political nation of Israel. However, we can learn important principles of justice from these laws.

---

[8] See Book 2, Chapter 20, Sections 14 and 15.
[9] See chapter 19.

c) The moral aspect

This included the universal unchangeable ethical principles. The Ten Commandments are a summary of the moral law, but the moral principles permeate the whole Old Testament. This aspect of the law was not changed in any way when Christ came. It reflects the character of God.

The following figure summarizes the change in the use of the three aspects of the Old Testament law:

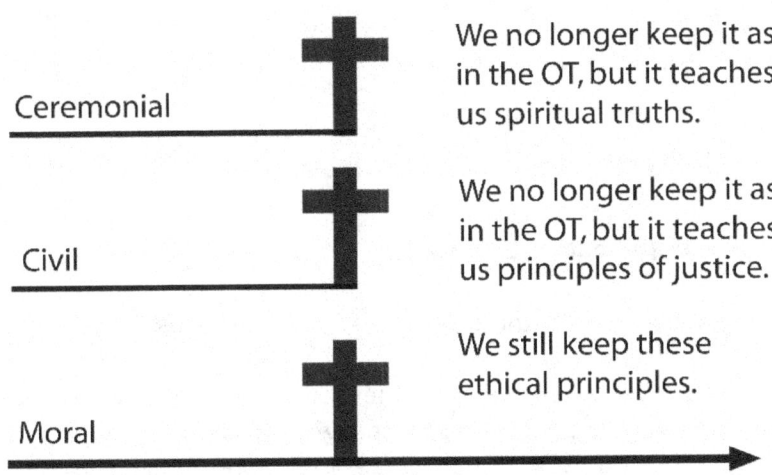

Ceremonial — We no longer keep it as in the OT, but it teaches us spiritual truths.

Civil — We no longer keep it as in the OT, but it teaches us principles of justice.

Moral — We still keep these ethical principles.

THE THREE ASPECTS OF THE OT LAW

The West*minster Confession of Faith* says the following:

> Beside this law, commonly called *moral*, God was pleased to give to the people of Israel, as a church under age, *ceremonial laws*, containing several typical ordinances, ...All which ceremonial laws are now

abrogated, under the new testament. ...To them also, as a body politic, he gave sundry *judicial laws*, which expired together with the State of that people;... (Chapter 19, sections 3 and 4)

For Review:

1. Describe the three aspects of the Old Testament law.

2. How did the application of each aspect change in the New Testament age?

F. Examples of Application

Punishments in Exodus 21

Going back to the examples found in Exodus 21 regarding the punishment for murder or for children who curse their parents, how should we apply these passages today? First, there is a moral aspect that hasn't changed: it is wrong to commit murder and it is wrong to curse your parents. Secondly, the punishments belong to the civil aspect of the law, meant only for the nation of Israel at that time. They show the seriousness of all sin, but we no longer need to carry out such strict and severe punishments. Finally, these laws point us to Christ. They remind us of His teaching that when we are angry, we have broken the commandment to not kill (Matthew 5:21-22). They also remind us that He took upon Himself the punishment we all deserve.

The Sabbatical Year and the Year of Jubilee

To see how this works, let's look at an example. How do we apply the teachings found in Leviticus 25 and Deuteronomy 15 regarding the Sabbatical Year and the Year of Jubilee? In these chapters, we read that on every seventh year (Sabbatical Year) they were to rest from cultivating the land (Leviticus 25:4), debts between the Jews were to be forgiven (Deuteronomy 15:1-2), and fellow Jews who had become poor and had sold themselves as servants were free to return to their families (Dt. 15:12). Every fiftieth year (The Year of Jubilee, after seven periods of seven years), properties that had been sold were to be returned to their original owner (Lev. 25:10). Notice that people could gain material benefits by taking initiative and working hard, but there were limits to how much and how long they could continue to multiply those benefits.

Consider the three aspects of this passage:

a) The civil aspect:
As a political entity, Israel had to supervise the management of property and economic affairs. However, since the people of God is no longer the nation of Israel and we aren't organized as a Christian nation, these civil laws don't need to be applied in the same way today.

Nevertheless, we do find helpful principles of justice. The laws of this passage reminded them that God was the real owner of their property. They provided an incentive for being diligent, but they also showed Israel how to practice mercy, justice, and compassion. Returning the land to its original owner every fifty years prevented people from piling up more and more riches, generation after generation, while others became more and more poor and dependent. It provided a new opportunity for those who had made mistakes, who had been sick or injured, who were affected adversely by bad weather, or who had for some other reason fallen into debt.

These are *principles* that can be incorporated into the laws of the countries where we live, without applying the laws literally in the same way as they were meant to be applied at that time. As Christians, we can work to see that our law-makers protect freedom and encourage initiative in our economic policies. But we can also encourage them to show mercy and compassion. We can vote for candidates who will put limits on the abuse of riches and power. The proper application of these principles of justice will vary in each country where Christians strive to influence for greater justice.

b) The ceremonial aspect:

The year of Jubilee began on the Day of Atonement with the sound of a loud trumpet (Lev. 25:9). This indicates a connection with the ceremonial aspect of the law, and points to Christ's atoning work.

We no longer need to keep this aspect of the laws, because Jesus already fulfilled them as He made the last sacrifice. However, we can profit greatly from a study of these passages and apply the spiritual truths to our lives. We can understand certain dimensions of our salvation better and grow in our gratefulness toward Christ. For example, treeing servants, forgiving debts, and proclaiming liberty represent liberation from our slavery to sin and forgiveness of our spiritual debt. Letting the land rest and trusting God to provide during those years symbolizes our spiritual rest in Christ, pointing to the fact that we are saved by faith and not by works.

c) The moral aspect:

There are certain universal and eternal moral principles found in these chapters that we should always apply. We already touched on some as we looked at the principles of justice found in the civil aspect of the law. We should always remember that our possessions belong to the Lord and that we should be generous with them. We should show mercy to the poor and needy. We should work diligently, but we should avoid piling up riches at the expense of others. Absolute economic equality is not the goal, but extreme and prolonged inequality should be restrained.

G. Developing a New Attitude

As mentioned previously, Paul provides the analogy of the difference between slaves and heirs in Galatians, chapters 3 and 4. This will help us develop a new attitude toward the Old Testament laws. While an heir is a child, it's hard to tell much difference between him and a young slave or a young servant. They are both told what to do, given specific orders, and punished when they disobey. For example, a father tells his child, "Don't touch the stove! Don't cross the street!" However, when they both grow up, you can see a big difference. The son is then given greater freedom along with greater responsibility, while the slave continues in his lower position. The father might tell his grown-up son, for example, "Take care of yourself!" The son is now more mature and allowed to apply the principles on his own. But he still gives the slave more detailed orders.

The point is that the Old Testament believers were heirs, but still children. As the *Westminster Confession of Faith* says, the nation of Israel was like an "under-age" church. Now, during the New Covenant age, God's people are more mature, so we are given greater freedom, but also greater responsibility.

Galatians 3:24-25
So then, the law was our guardian until Christ came, in order that we might be justified by faith. But now that faith has come, we are no longer under a guardian.

Galatians 4:1-5
I mean that the heir, as long as he is a child, is no different from a slave, though he is the owner of everything, but he is under guardians and managers until the date set by his father. In the same way we also, when we were children, were enslaved to the elementary principles of the world. But when the fullness of time had come, God sent forth his Son, born of woman, born under the law, to redeem those who were under the law, so that we might receive adoption as sons.

**The People of
God in the O.T.**   **The People of
God in the N.T.**

Calvin uses an illustration in his commentary on Galatians 3:23 to explain this change of the New Testament. It's also helpful for understanding what our attitude should be toward the Old Testament law. He says the Old Testament people were walking on the same road as the New Testament believers, but they started out at dawn, and now it is noonday.

> Whatever might be the amount of darkness under the law, the fathers were not ignorant of the road in which they ought to walk. Though the law is not equal to the splendor of noon, yet, as it is sufficient to direct a journey, travelers do not wait till the sun is fully risen. Their portion of light resembled the dawn, which was enough to preserve them from all error, and guide them to everlasting blessedness.

Conclusion

We can discern three different aspects of the Old Testament law: ceremonial, civil, and moral. Since Jesus has made the final sacrifice, we no longer practice the ceremonies. Since God's people is no longer the nation of Israel, we no longer keep the civil law as they were expected to in the period of the Old Testament, especially the punishments. However, the moral principles of the law remain valid for all people in all times. Also, it is profitable to study even the ceremonial and civil aspects of the law. The ethical basis of the law has not changed, but the application of the ceremonial and civil aspects has changed.

Seeking the universal ethical principles may not always be easy, but we are no longer children, and we have been given greater grace in the New Testament age to apply the principles as adults. We are on the same road as our Old Testament fathers, but the light is brighter. The people of God are no longer like a child holding the hand of a tutor who is taking us to Christ; we now hold the hand of the Master Himself.

For Review:

1. How should we apply the passages about punishments in Exodus 21?

2. How should we apply the teachings found in Leviticus 25 and Deuteronomy 15 regarding the Sabbatical Year and the Year of Jubilee?

3. What is the analogy used by Paul in Galatians 3 and 4 to show the difference between the people of God in the Old Testament and the people of God in the New Testament?

4. What is the analogy used by Calvin to show the contrast between the people of God in the Old Testament and the people of God in the New Testament, especially regarding their use of the law.

The Essential Point
We no longer keep the ceremonial and civil aspects of the Old Testament law in the same way as before Christ, but we do keep the moral aspect.

Personal Application

a) Bible Study

Study Galatians 4:1-7. What does this passage teach about the difference between the people of God in the Old Testament and the people of God now in the New Testament age? What does this mean for you personally?

b) Prayer

Use Psalm 119:1-16 as a guide for your prayer time. Ask the Lord for wisdom to use the Scriptures correctly.

c) Memorization of Scripture

Galatians 3:24-25
So then, the law was our guardian until Christ came, in order that we might be justified by faith. But now that faith has come, we are no longer under a guardian.

Galatians 4:4-5
But when the fullness of time had come, God sent forth his Son, born of woman, born under the law, to redeem those who were under the law, so that we might receive adoption as sons.

For Further Reflection and Discussion:

1. How has this chapter changed your attitude toward the Old Testament law? Has it been helpful?

2. Consider other passages of Old Testament law. Try to identify the ceremonial, civil, and moral aspects. Analyze how we should keep these laws today. See, for example, Leviticus 19:28 or Leviticus 20:13.

4. How Can I Avoid Spiritual Dryness?

"Holiness hardly ever becomes a reality
until we care more about Jesus than about holiness."

(Stephen Brown, *A Scandalous Freedom*)

Introduction

In *The Pilgrim's Regress* by C.S. Lewis, the narrator recounts his dream of a boy from Puritania who receives a big card from the "Steward" with a long list of all the things he should not do. Half the rules forbid things he had never heard of, and the other half were things he was already doing every day. "The number of rules was so enormous that he felt he could never remember them all." The card said "you must be always examining yourself to see how many rules you had broken."[10] I think this represents the way some people feel about Christianity. When I was in Chile, the first question people often asked me when they heard I was a missionary was, "what does your church forbid?"

Some Christians try so hard to *make themselves holy* that they take their eyes off Jesus and lose their joy. They dry up spiritually. This is what happened to the believers in Galatia. False teachers had led them astray, making them think they had to be circumcised and keep the Jewish customs of the Old Testament.[11] Paul tells them they should keep their focus on Christ and asks them, "Where is that joyful and grateful spirit you felt then?" (Galatians 4:15, NLT)

Christian growth is like growing a garden: I can't just sit on my couch and wait for God to make me a pretty garden, without sowing seeds, watering the plants, pruning and fertilizing. But the results are not in my control. I can't decide the color of the flowers, the height of the plants, and the number of leaves they have. The same principle applies to Christian growth. We should do whatever the Lord tells us, but trust Him for the results.

---

[10] C.S. Lewis. *The Pilgrim's Regress* in *The Timeless Writings of C.S. Lewis* (New York: Inspirational Press), pp. 5-6.

[11] We will deal with the subject of keeping the Old Testament laws in another chapter.

There are two ditches we can easily slide into on both sides of the Christian road of spiritual growth: legalism and libertinism. *Both lead to drying up spiritually*. In the first ditch, the person depends on human effort and focuses on the law, rather than depending on the Holy Spirit. The problem is that legalism doesn't really accomplish true sanctification; it only makes you tired and discouraged. In the second ditch, the person doesn't take God's commandments seriously. This will lead you farther and farther from God. We are called to love God, follow His will, and seek to become more like Christ.

In this chapter, we will explore the pitfalls of legalism and libertinism, then mention the tools that God has given us for our spiritual growth. We will highlight the importance of keeping your eyes on Jesus and the joy of living like children of God.

A. Avoid Legalism; Don't Focus on the Law.

When I was a child, I imagined God watching me from behind two huge tablets of the Ten Commandments, waiting to see if I committed a sin. I knew that Jesus had died on the cross to forgive my sins, but in my daily life, I focused on the law more than on Christ.

We looked at this in other chapters, but it can't be emphasized too much: in Galatians 3:23-4:7, Paul explains that the law was like a "guardian" to lead us to Christ. Unfortunately, many Jews began to focus on the law and trust their own works for salvation.

Romans 9:31-32
But Israel, who *pursued a law of righteousness*, has not attained it. Why not? Because they pursued it not by faith

but as if it were by works. They stumbled over the "stumbling stone."

They began to see the law in the foreground. Now, after Christ has come, we can look back at the cross and see Christ in the foreground. We don't discard the law, but the two tablets are now in the background, behind the cross. Now we see the law in the shadow of Christ.

The Law

Legalistic Perspective
Focus on the Law

Focus on Christ

When I drive down the highway in my car, I need to look at the signs to arrive at my destination safely. They tell me the speed limit, warn me about steep curves, and provide helpful information about the location of cities, gas stations, and places to eat. However, if I fix my gaze only on the signs, and take my eyes off the road, I'll have an accident! The law in the Bible works that way; it's a sign pointing us to Christ, and we should not give so much attention to it that we take our eyes off Him. Why do we sometimes focus on the law? It's because of our pride; we like to think we can do things on our own.

Paul reminds the Galatians that they should continue their Christian life by faith, not by human effort.

Galatians 3:3

Are you so foolish? Having begun by the Spirit, are you now being perfected by the flesh?

I like to fix things around the house, but I have a problem; when something doesn't work, I usually just try harder. If a screw doesn't go in right, I just push harder and try to force it. Sometimes the screw pops out, or maybe I cut my hand. Brute force doesn't work very well.

A good golfer knows that he can't simply hit the ball as hard as possible. He needs to hit the ball squarely with the appropriate force, pointed in the right direction. The Christian life is like that; instead of just trying harder, we need to learn what it means to grow by grace. It's true that there are no simple formulas for spiritual growth, and we spend our lives learning more about this. Nevertheless, I would like to suggest some principles that should be helpful.

For Review:

1. What is the mistake of legalism in its view of the law?

2. What is the solution to this mistake?

B. Don't Add to the Bible.

Another manifestation of legalism is to add to the ethical norms in Scripture. Historically, the Protestant church has fought ferociously for the freedom of conscience. In England, when certain customs or doctrines were being imposed, especially related to worship, the Protestants rebelled. When they wrote the *Westminster Confession of Faith*, they included chapter 20, "Of Christian Liberty and Liberty of Conscience."

> God alone is Lord of the conscience, and hath left it free from the doctrines and commandments of men, which are, in anything, contrary to His Word; or beside it, if matters of faith, or worship. So that, to believe such doctrines, or to obey such commands, out of conscience, is to betray true liberty of conscience: and the requiring of an implicit faith, and an absolute and blind obedience, is to destroy liberty of conscience, and reason also. (Section 2)

But the confession also explains that this freedom should not be confused with libertinism.

> They who, upon pretense of Christian liberty, do practice any sin, or cherish any lust, do thereby destroy the end of Christian liberty, which is, that being delivered out of the hands of our enemies, we might serve the Lord without fear, in holiness and righteousness before Him, all the days of our life. (Section 3)

The idea is that we should obey the norms in Scripture, but where the Bible does not speak, there is freedom.

The Bible clearly teaches that we should not add commandments to the Word of God.

Deuteronomy 4:2
You shall not add to the word that I command you, nor take from it, that you may keep the commandments of the LORD

your God that I command you. (See also Deuteronomy 12:32.)

Jesus harshly criticized the Pharisees for adding commandments to the Word of God.

Matthew 15:7-9
You hypocrites! Well did Isaiah prophesy of you, when he said: "This people honors me with their lips, but their heart is far from me; in vain do they worship me, teaching as doctrines the commandments of men." (See also Luke 11:46.)

Paul also warns against human regulations.

Colossians 2:20-23
If with Christ you died to the elemental spirits of the world, why, as if you were still alive in the world, do you submit to regulations— "Do not handle, Do not taste, Do not touch" (referring to things that all perish as they are used)— according to human precepts and teachings? These have indeed an appearance of wisdom in promoting self-made religion and asceticism and severity to the body, but they are of no value in stopping the indulgence of the flesh.

Some people tend to be stricter than the Bible itself in order to obtain holiness. They think people will always deviate from the norm, so it's better to make rules that are stricter than the Bible. This way, when people loosen their stance, they will still be within the biblical parameters. But this is not a biblical view. It comes from trusting human efforts instead of trusting God.

Suppose a pastor has seen problems with drugs and decides to teach that the Bible forbids using any kind of drugs, including what doctors prescribe. The result could be that someone dies because they didn't take the proper medicine!

The fact that there are many car accidents doesn't justify forbidding the use of cars. Instead of avoiding cars altogether, we should learn to use them properly.

The Lord put His own regulations in the Bible just the way He wanted them. We shouldn't change them, take away from them or add to them!

2 Timothy 3:16-17
All Scripture is breathed out by God and profitable for teaching, for reproof, for correction, and for training in righteousness, that the man of God may be complete, equipped for every good work.

This doesn't mean there has to be a specific or detailed statement; it could be teachings from which we draw applications. For example, the command to not steal doesn't include a list of specific ways you shouldn't steal. You can easily conclude that you shouldn't steal money from the cash box at work!

For Review:

What is the biblical support for avoiding adding commandments to the Word of God? Mention some key passages.

C. Avoid Libertinism

As we free ourselves from legalism, we might stumble over into the ditch of libertinism on the other side of the road. But Christian liberty does not mean we can just live any way we wish.

In Galatians 5:13, Paul says:

> For you were called to freedom, brothers. Only do not use your freedom as an opportunity for the flesh, but through love serve one another.

James wrote his letter to correct a misunderstanding of salvation by faith. He insists that true faith will produce changes in our lives. Otherwise, it is actually "dead" faith (James 2:17-26). The Bible contains countless moral exhortations. When Jesus changes our hearts, He gives us a desire to please Him with our lives. He said, "If you love me, you will keep my commandments" (John 14:15).

Paul warns us in 1 Timothy 3 that in the last days, things will become more difficult. People will become "lovers of self, lovers of money, proud, arrogant, and abusive." Sometimes the evil in the world can also spill over into the church. That is why we are told to pray, "and lead us not into temptation, but deliver us from evil" (Matthew 6:13).

For those who have come from a legalistic background, it might help to remember that Jesus did not sum up the law by saying, "be good!" Rather, He said the greatest commandment is to *love God*, and the second is to *love your neighbor* as yourself (Matthew 22:26-40). Furthermore, following God's principles is beneficial for us and the whole world.

There is an evangelistic tract called "The Two Brothers." It tells about a murderer who is sentenced to death. His brother, who was a very good person, loved him so much that he dressed in his clothes and went to die in his place. He left his own clothes with a note for the one who had been condemned to die, that said, "My dear brother, I took your place today. I only ask one thing of you, that you put on my clothes and live the kind of life I was living."

That's what Jesus has done for us: He died in our place, so that could be free from condemnation and so that we could begin a new life. *Now he asks us to put on His character and live our lives the way He would.*

D. Becoming More Like Jesus

What can we do to grow spiritually and become more like Jesus? We already know we can't just "try harder," but what should we do then?

1) Use the means of grace.

First, we should use the means of grace that God has given us: the Word, prayer, Christian fellowship, and the sacraments. If we don't use them, we can't expect to grow.

It's like the joke about the man who climbed the roof of his house in a flood and prayed for help. Soon a boat came by offering to take him to dry land. He answered, "No, thanks, I'm waiting for God to save me." Then a helicopter came, and again, he refused their help because he was "trusting God." Finally, he drowned and went to heaven. He asked God, rather upset, "Why didn't you help me?" God answered that he had sent him a boat and a helicopter, but that he had refused to accept His help!

93

But we should be careful; the temptation is to think that the mere act of practicing the spiritual disciplines means we will grow. Then we take our eyes off Christ and lose connection with the true source of spiritual power .

For Review:

1. What are the means of grace?

2. How should we use them?

2) Practice repentance.

Proverbs 4:23 says we should "keep our heart with all vigilance," because it is the center of our life, values and character. The first step toward developing a healthy heart is being honest, especially with ourselves. We have to stop deceiving ourselves, thinking that we have reached a high level of spirituality. The truth is that we are very far from our goal of becoming like Christ. We are self-centered, envious, fearful, impure, and arrogant.

> Romans 12:3
> For by the grace given to me I say to everyone among you not to think of himself more highly than he ought to think, but to think with sober judgment, each according to the measure of faith that God has assigned.

This self-deception of thinking we are doing so well develops this way: 1) When we are children, we don't receive perfect unconditional love, not even from our parents, because nobody is perfect. 2) We begin to think we should act or be a certain way, or that we should accomplish certain things, in order to be loved. Maybe we think we should always be kind, never lie, never become angry, and never complain. 3) We build an image of ourselves that fits what we think we *should be*. 4) Finally, we begin to believe that we *really are* like that image, even though it isn't true. It's because we desire to be loved, and don't want to suffer the pain of rejection.[12]

The problem is that in this way we have a hard time admitting our real problems, and therefore we don't solve them either. Maybe we are angry with somebody, but refuse to admit it, even to ourselves. God desires honesty in the innermost part of our hearts. This is called "integrity." Psalm 51:6 says, "Behold, you delight in truth in the inward being...." Psalm 32:3-4 explains what happens when we don't admit our sins:

> For when I kept silent, my bones wasted away through my groaning all day long. For day and night your hand was heavy upon me; my strength was dried up as by the heat of summer.

It becomes unbearable! On the other hand, when we confess our sin, there is a joyful relief:

> Psalm 32:1-2, 5, 11
> Blessed is the one whose transgression is forgiven, whose sin is covered. Blessed is the man against whom the LORD counts no iniquity, and in whose spirit there is no deceit.
> ...I acknowledged my sin to you, and I did not cover my iniquity; I said, "I will confess my transgressions to the LORD," and you forgave the iniquity of my sin.

---

[12] See David Seamonds, *Healing Grace* (Indianapolis, IN: Light & Life Communications, 1999) for a good explanation of this process.

...Be glad in the LORD, and rejoice, O righteous, and shout for joy, all you upright in heart!

We should practice repentance daily, because we sin daily in our attitudes, motives, thoughts and actions. The worst sins are in our hearts, like arrogance, envy, resentment, and self-centeredness.

The apostle Paul thought he was doing well, until he understood the tenth commandment about coveting. In Romans 7, he explains the process of repentance. He becomes aware that there is something inside him that he can't control, a negative force that he can't dominate. He concludes that it is sin. He ends the chapter by calling out to the Lord, asking for His help.

Romans 7:19-25
For I do not do the good I want, but the evil I do not want is what I keep on doing. Now if I do what I do not want, it is no longer I who do it, but sin that dwells within me. So I find it to be a law that when I want to do right, evil lies close at hand. For I delight in the law of God, in my inner being, but I see in my members another law waging war against the law of my mind and making me captive to the law of sin that dwells in my members. Wretched man that I am! Who will deliver me from this body of death? Thanks be to God through Jesus Christ our Lord! So then, I myself serve the law of God with my mind, but with my flesh I serve the law of sin.

As Dr. C. John Miller taught, the more we recognize our sin, the bigger we see Christ. [13]

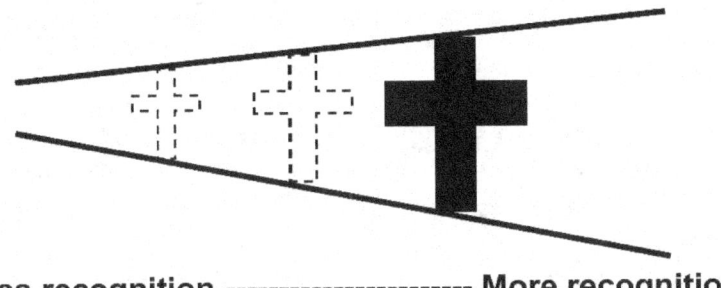

Less recognition ----------------------- More recognition

Repentance is not the same as "penance," where supposedly the person has to do something to cover his or her sin to avoid temporal punishment. Forgiveness is free. Repentance means recognizing our sin and asking for forgiveness. It also means turning from sin to Christ. It is a change of heart.

> 1 John 1:8-10
> If we say we have no sin, we deceive ourselves, and the truth is not in us. If we confess our sins, he is faithful and just to forgive us our sins and to cleanse us from all unrighteousness. If we say we have not sinned, we make him a liar, and his word is not in us.

I love the figure of Jesus washing the disciples' feet in John 13. Normally, this passage is cited to talk about service, and of course this is an important application of the text. Nevertheless, I think the central theme is *forgiveness*. Washing symbolizes the

---

[13] I first heard this presented by my friend, Rev. Ronald Lutz in a "Sonship" seminar.

greatest service we can offer: forgiving someone who has offended us. When Peter refuses this service, Jesus insists. He says if he doesn't let Him wash His feet, he has nothing to do with Him. Why does Jesus state this so strongly? Notice that when Peter wants to be washed completely, Jesus tells him they are already clean, but not all of them. I conclude that He is talking about the cleansing of forgiveness. When we think of it this way, Jesus' attitude is very moving: He really *wants* to forgive us! He *enjoys* forgiving us! In His mercy, He takes the initiative and *insists* on forgiving us! When we recognize the depth of our sin, we can also recognize the abundance of His grace.

For Review:

What is repentance?

3) Keep your eyes on Jesus.

To grow spiritually, without making it seem like a burden, we need to fix our eyes on Jesus, who both gives us faith in the beginning and strengthens our faith as we continue. When we take our eyes off Him, we lose our way. If we look at others, or if we look at ourselves, we stumble and fall.

Hebrews 12:1-2
Therefore, since we are surrounded by so great a cloud of witnesses, let us also lay aside every weight, and sin which clings so closely, and let us run with endurance the race that is set before us, looking to Jesus, the founder and perfecter of our faith, who for the joy that was set before

him endured the cross, despising the shame, and is seated at the right hand of the throne of God.

It's curious how growing by grace works. It almost happens without realizing it, because we stop thinking so much about ourselves, and we think more about Christ. If someone tries hard to grow, and is too conscious of his own spiritual situation, he is looking too much at himself, which only impedes growth. On the other hand, if he focuses on the Lord, he begins to become more like Him. It's like a child who becomes more like his father or her mother, without making a conscious effort to do so. He simply follows their example instinctively. This is the way it happens in our spiritual development.

2 Corinthians 3:18
And we all, with unveiled face, beholding the glory of the Lord, are being transformed into the same image from one degree of glory to another. For this comes from the Lord who is the Spirit.

Keeping your eyes on the Lord means depending totally on Him. We use the means of grace, but we trust *Him* for their efficacy. Jesus teaches us in John 15 that without Him, we can do nothing, but if we remain in Him, we will bear much fruit.

John 15:5
I am the vine; you are the branches. Whoever abides in me and I in him, he it is that bears much fruit, for apart from me you can do nothing.

We should be like a deep-sea diver, with an oxygen hose connected at every moment, and not like a scuba diver, who uses oxygen tanks and returns once in a while to get more. Our dependence is continual. That way we can also swim in deeper water when necessary.

For Review:

What is the lesson from Hebrews 12:1-2 regarding spiritual growth?

4) Live as sons and daughters, not as slaves.

Another key to enjoying our spiritual growth is to remember that we are children of God, not slaves. In addition to the passage in Galatians 3 and 4 that we have already considered, there are other passages that emphasize our status as children of God.

Romans 8:14,15
For all who are led by the Spirit of God are sons of God. For you did not receive the spirit of slavery to fall back into fear, but you have received the Spirit of adoption as sons, by whom we cry, "Abba! Father!"

A slave is the property of his owner, while a son or daughter belongs to the family. Slaves don't have a right to inherit anything, but children receive the family possessions. A slave does not have the privilege of going to talk to his owner whenever he wants, but a child can count on his parents to give him time. A slave is punished to correct his conduct, but children are disciplined out of love for their own good.

Hebrews 12:6
For the Lord disciplines the one he loves, and chastises every son whom he receives.

As God's children, we trust Him to work things out for our own good. We want to obey out of love, not because of fear. We have joy in our relationship with God, and we are not simply trying to do our duty with a bitter and resentful attitude. Our sanctification comes from the "inside out," and not from the outside in.[14]

Augustine said, "Love and do as thou wilt."[15] At first reading, this sounds terribly wrong. However, after analyzing it somewhat, it makes sense; it just needs to be explained properly. First, if in any moment we are really loving God and loving our neighbor, we will want to do what is right and our actions will show it. On the other hand, if we are not loving God and our neighbor, this produces sin. Secondly, when we are born again, we experience a change of heart. Now at the very center of our being, we really want to do God's will.

Romans 7:22
For I delight in the law of God, in my inner being.

Of course, sometimes when temptation overcomes us, we momentarily desire to sin, but when this happens, we aren't happy about it. This is the struggle that Paul describes in Romans 7. Deep in our heart, we want to please God, and we cry out,

---

[14] See Larry Crabb, *Inside Out* (Colorado Springs: NavPress, 1988).
[15] Philip Schaff: NPNF1-07. St. Augustine: Homilies on the Gospel of John; Homilies on the First Epistle of John; Soliloquies - Christian Classics Ethereal Library <www.ccel.org> (06/01/2021)

"Wretched man that I am! Who will deliver me from this body of death?" (Romans 7:24)

I am intrigued by what I have read about the difference between the two great Russian writers, Leon Tolstoy and Fyodor Dostoyevsky. Neither one was exactly a saint, but they both considered themselves Christians. Tolstoy really tried to fulfill the demands of the Scriptures, but he seemed to always feel guilty. He wrote a letter saying he was "guilty and vile, worthy of being despised." He became so discouraged that he had all the ropes and arms in his house hidden from him so that he wouldn't kill himself. He finally ran away from home, lived like a vagabond, and eventually died in a train station.

On the other hand, Dostoyevsky apparently had a better comprehension of the grace of God. He was almost killed by a firing squad along with a group of radicals, but at the last moment, they fired into the air. After that traumatic incident, while some died and others went crazy, Dostoyevsky felt he had been born again. When he was boarding the train to go to prison in Siberia, a woman handed him a New Testament with some money stashed between the pages. The money didn't help much, but the Scriptures changed his life, and the New Testament was never far from him the rest of his life. He had nothing else to read in prison, and before he was released, he became a free man spiritually. He wrote the following creed in prison:

> I believe that there is nothing more beautiful, more profound, more compassionate, more reasonable, more valuable and more perfect than Christ. And not only is there nothing, but I say to myself with a jealous love, that there never could be.

On his deathbed, he summoned his wife and his children. He asked his wife to read the story of the prodigal son from the Bible. Then he said:

> My children, never forget what you have just heard. Have absolute faith in God, and never doubt His forgiveness. I love you profoundly, but my love is nothing compared to the love of God. Even if you commit a horrendous crime and feel only bitterness, do not stray from God. You are His children. Humble yourselves before Him as before a father; plead for His forgiveness, and he will rejoice in your repentance, as a father rejoiced in his prodigal son. [16]

A few minutes later, he died.

This should be the guideline for our relationship with God: we are His prodigal sons and daughters who have come back home. We wandered away from God and were living a miserable life among the "pigs." But our loving heavenly Father was waiting for us to return, and He ran to receive us with open arms. Now we are home again, and we should live like His children, not like slaves.

For Review:

What should we focus on when we consider our relationship with God?

---

[16] See Philip Yancey, *The Jesus I Never Knew*, (Grand Rapids: Zondervan, 1995), and Ruth Bell Graham, *Prodigals and Those Who Love Them* (Colorado Springs, Colorado: Focus on the Family, 1991), pp. 119-126.

The Essential Points

1. Avoid the pitfalls of legalism and libertinism.
2. Use the means of grace and practice repentance.
3. Keep your eyes on Jesus and live like children of God.

For Personal Application

a) Bible Study

For this chapter, study Galatians 3:23-4:7.

b) Prayer

Use John 14:26-27 to guide your prayer time.

c) Memorization of Scripture

Hebrews 12:1b-2a
Let us run with endurance the race that is set before us, looking to Jesus, the founder and perfecter of our faith.

Romans 8:14,15
For all who are led by the Spirit of God are sons of God. For you did not receive the spirit of slavery to fall back into fear, but you have received the Spirit of adoption as sons, by whom we cry, "Abba! Father!"

For Further Reflection and Discussion:

1. What advice would you give to the young man who stayed home to avoid temptations?

2. What is the most common tendency among Christians you know? Do they tend to be passive and indifferent about sanctification? Or do they tend to be legalistic, trying to sanctify themselves by their own effort? How about you? What is your tendency? What can you do to avoid it?

3. Are you using the means of grace on a regular basis? How could you improve your use of them?

4. Do you identify more with Tolstoy or with Dostoyevsky? Explain why.

5. If God Plans Everything, Do I Have Free Will?

"The great act of faith is when man decides he is not God."

Oliver Wendell Holmes junior, letter

Introduction

I remember the first time I began to believe that every detail of my whole life was being governed by God. It gave me a sense of joy and peace that I had never experienced before. It was a great relief to know that if something didn't go the way I had hoped, there was a reason for it; God had a better plan. This was during my college years, and I remember thinking, if I am late for my early class because the alarm didn't work, instead of fretting about it all day, I can relax, knowing that maybe God had saved me from having an accident or some other problem. I didn't need to know why, but I knew it was OK. *Everything* was OK!

However, I struggled with what this meant for my own responsibility. Obviously, God doesn't want me to be passive. I can't stop studying, then ask God to help me pass my courses. Just how much is my part and how much is God's part? Is it 50% God's and 50% mine? How about prayer? Why should I pray if God has planned everything and controls everything anyway?

There are two extremes to avoid. On the one hand, if we really believe that God plans and controls everything, we might be tempted to become passive, making no effort to solve problems or help people who are suffering. Why even try? There is nothing I can do to change things. In fact, we might be tempted to think of ourselves as mere puppets. On the other hand, if we reject the idea that God plans and controls everything, we might begin to feel anxious about everything. If God is not in control, who is? Maybe it depends on me. If God is not in control, is He really God?

Let's look at the biblical teachings on this subject. There must be some way to harmonize the teachings of God's sovereign control with human freedom and responsibility. There must be a way to avoid becoming a puppet without denying who God really is. There must be a way to believe that I can choose which train to get on, without facing uncertainty like the traveler in "The Switchman" story.

A. Sovereignty, Predestination and Providence

The Bible teaches clearly that God plans everything and governs everything that happens. There is nothing that escapes His control. I have never really questioned this doctrine, because it seems like an essential aspect of His nature. He wouldn't be God otherwise.

We say God is "sovereign," referring to His role as supreme ruler of the universe. We say that He "predestined" everything, meaning that He planned everything from eternity. Since He is sovereign, whatever He planned will happen. Often people use the word "predestination" to refer specifically to the teaching that God predetermines who will be saved, but it can also refer to *determining everything*. When we speak of God's "providence," we are considering His continual care over all things. God's providence is His way of making sure that His plans are fulfilled.

Consider how the following passages teach these three truths:

a. God is *sovereign*.

> Psalm 115:3
> Our God is in the heavens; he does all that he pleases.

> Daniel 4:35
> All the inhabitants of the earth are accounted as nothing, and he does according to his will among the host of heaven and among the inhabitants of the earth; and none can stay his hand or say to him, "What have you done?"

b. He has *predestined* everything, even the smallest events.

> Ephesians 1:11
> In him we have obtained an inheritance, having been predestined according to the purpose of him who works all things according to the counsel of his will.

> Proverbs 16:33
> The lot is cast into the lap, but its every decision is from the LORD.

c. His *providence* brings about the fulfillment of everything He has predestined.

> Isaiah 14:24
> The LORD of hosts has sworn: "As I have planned, so shall it be, and as I have purposed, so shall it stand."

> Isaiah 46:9-11
> Remember the former things of old; for I am God, and there is no other; I am God, and there is none like me, declaring the end from the beginning and from ancient

times things not yet done, saying, 'My counsel shall stand, and I will accomplish all my purpose,' calling a bird of prey from the east, the man of my counsel from a far country. I have spoken, and I will bring it to pass; I have purposed, and I will do it.

It's clear, isn't it? Nobody can change His plans. Absolutely everything happens according to His will. If God were not in control of everything, He wouldn't be God! How would you feel if you realized you were flying in a plane without a pilot at the controls? How would you feel if you thought God was not in control of the universe?

The *Westminster Confession of Faith* explains these three aspects:

Sovereignty:
He is the alone foundation of all being, of whom, through whom, and to whom, are all things; and hath most sovereign dominion over them, to do by them, for them, or upon them, whatsoever Himself pleaseth. (Chapter II, Section 2)

Predestination:
God from all eternity did by the most wise and holy counsel of His own will, freely and unchangeably ordain whatsoever comes to pass. (Chapter III, Section 1)

Providence:
God, the great Creator of all things, doth uphold, direct dispose, and govern all creatures, actions, and things, from the greatest even to the least, by His most wise and holy providence, according to His infallible foreknowledge, and the free and immutable counsel of His own will, to the

praise of the glory of His wisdom, power, justice, goodness, and mercy. (Chapter V, Section 1).[17]

For Review:

1. What are the problems we face in understanding the relation between God's sovereignty and man's responsibility?

2. Explain the meaning of "sovereignty," "predestination," and "providence."

3. Mention key Bible passages that support these three concepts.

B. The Freedom and Responsibility of Man

The problem is that these teachings could make us feel like we are not really free, that we just respond mechanically to the movements of God's hands. However, it's not like that. Until now, we have seen only one side of the biblical teaching.

The other side is that man is a responsible being, having his own will to make decisions. This is just as intuitively apparent as the sovereignty of God. If man is not free to make decisions, he is not really man; he is not the image of God. It's also clearly taught in the Bible. From the beginning we see that human beings are responsible for their decisions and their actions: Adam and Eve were cast out of the Garden of Eden because of their sin (Genesis 3).

---

[17] See https://westminsterstandards.org/westminster-confession-of-faith/

One of the most amazing things that God gave man was freedom to think and make decisions. Adam and Eve could have chosen to obey or to disobey. Of course, human freedom was never without limits; we can't jump to the moon or run on foot at 1,000 miles an hour. We are talking about the freedom to exercise our will to make decisions.

After the Fall, man's capacity to make decisions became damaged. He is incapable of choosing good without God's help. He can't choose to believe in Christ until the Holy Spirit changes his heart. He still has a will, and he still makes choices, but he is inclined toward sin. Although he can do deeds that outwardly can be considered "good," when we consider the motives of the heart, even those deeds are not pleasing to God.

Genesis 6:5
The LORD saw that the wickedness of man was great in the earth, and that every intention of the thoughts of his heart was only evil continually.

Hebrews 11:6
And without faith it is impossible to please him.

James M. Boice uses the illustration of an animal that by its nature eats only meat. If we offer him herbs, he won't eat them. Is he free to eat them? Yes, but he doesn't want to. Man is like that after the Fall; he is free to make his own decisions, but his nature has been so affected by the Fall that he prefers to choose what is wrong.[18]

We should clarify that God, in His mercy, restrains the effects of sin and helps all kinds of people, even non-believers,

---

[18] James Montgomery Boice, *Foundations of the Christian Faith* (Downers Grove, IL: InterVarsity Press, 1986), 210.

enabling them to do things that are good, in spite of their human inclination. This is not their merit, but God's. Theologians call this "common grace" or "universal grace." We receive the benefits of this grace every day for our food and clothing, for our health and housing, for beautiful art and music.

Also, the wonderful thing is that after the Holy Spirit changes our hearts and we put our faith in Christ, we are truly free again. Sin is no longer our master (Romans 6.14). Our new nature allows us to want good and choose good. Again, this is not our merit, but the Lord's. But the more we grow spiritually, the more it becomes the inclination of our heart.

Jonathan Edwards made the distinction between "natural" freedom and "moral" freedom. Natural freedom means we are free to act in accordance with our desires, and moral freedom means we are able to do good. He says before the Fall, man had both natural freedom and moral freedom. After the fall, he has natural freedom but not moral freedom. When he becomes a Christian, he again has both natural freedom and moral freedom.[19]

The Christian view is not like the deistic concept of a god who created everything and left it running like a machine or left it evolving as a huge organism. Neither is it like the fatalistic perspective of some Muslims who believe Allah is continually creating and recreating the atoms of everything, including man's own mind, to control everything, while giving man only the impression of free will.[20]

---

[19] Boice explains Edwards' view, taken from *Freedom of the Will,* in *Foundations of the Christian Faith,* 211–16.

[20] J. N. D. Anderson, *The World's Religions* (Grand Rapids: Eerdmans, 1968), 74.

C. Harmonizing God's Providence with Man's Freedom

But we still have a theological problem: The difficulty is in reconciling man's freedom with the doctrine of providence. How can man really be free to make a choice if all things happen according to God's sovereign will? Is our freedom only an illusion? It certainly seems like we have freedom to think our own thoughts and make our own decisions. We don't see ourselves as puppets who simply respond to God in a mechanical way. So we need to find a way to harmonize the two teachings of divine providence and human freedom. Here are some thoughts that help me:

1. Two Perspectives of Events

It would be pretentious to think we can fully grasp how to harmonize God's providence and man's freedom. However, it may help to think of two perspectives. One is like looking at things from far away through a *telescope*, and the other is like looking up close through a *microscope*.

From one perspective, we see that God plans everything and carries out His plan. This is the view through a telescope from far away. It's the big picture. God lives beyond time and space, so for Him, all of earth's history is like a moment within eternity.

2 Peter 3:8
But do not overlook this one fact, beloved, that with the Lord one day is as a thousand years, and a thousand years as one day.

From another perspective, man is inserted in time and history, living each moment in succession. He exercises his own will to make decisions, and his decisions change the course of history. This is like looking at things from close up, through a microscope, observing the details.

On the one hand, if the Lord did not show us the larger perspective, the only view we would have would be the smaller one. This would diminish the grandeur of God, and we would have less trust in Him. On the other hand, if the Lord did not show us the smaller perspective, we would possibly become fatalistic and passive. God has shown us both the big picture and the smaller picture, so that we give Him the glory and so that we act responsibly.

Prayer is a truly mysterious exercise where we show that we believe both of these truths that are difficult to reconcile. In prayer we practice both God's sovereignty and man's responsibility. On the one hand, prayer shows we trust God as sovereign. If He didn't control everything, how could we trust Him to answer our prayer? On the other hand, prayer shows we believe that our participation is somehow an important part of the development of God's plan. We wouldn't pray at all if we thought it didn't make any difference.

Man, with his limited mind, can't comprehend exactly how these two perspectives fit together. Nevertheless, both truths seem unavoidable, and we know that in the infinite mind of God, they are perfectly harmonized.

The fact that we are not able to understand something as well as we would like shouldn't keep us from believing that it is true. We accept many things that we don't understand, at least not yet. We can't really comprehend how God could be one God and three persons at the same time, but it doesn't mean it isn't true. We acknowledge human emotions without understanding very well how they function. There are concepts like eternity and infinity that we speak of, knowing that they escape our comprehension. We accept the fact that the universe apparently has no end. We can't really grasp it, but it seems like it can't be any other way.

When I was a young boy, we would travel twenty miles to go to church twice every Sunday, once in the morning and once at night. On the way back at night I liked to lean my head back and look at the multitude of bright stars through the back window. I can remember the moment when I realized that space had no roof on it. I was trying to imagine as far out as possible, wondering what it would be like. First, I imagined a huge wall, like a roof over the sky above the stars, but then I suddenly realized that it couldn't be the end. I thought to myself, "If there's a wall, then something must be on the other side of the wall, and there would be more space over there, so it must just go on and on!" I kept thinking about the size of the universe, totally amazed to realize that it had no end, but still unable to grasp the concept.

In the same way, we know that God is controlling everything that occurs and we also know that we are free to make decisions, without seeing exactly how they fit together. On the one hand, if God doesn't control everything, He wouldn't be God. We can't completely understand providence, but how could we believe it's NOT true?! On the other hand, if man didn't make decisions, he wouldn't be man! Again, we can't completely understand freedom, but we know we have it. How could we believe it's NOT true?!

Isaiah 55:8
For my thoughts are not your thoughts, neither are your ways my ways, declares the LORD.

Romans 11:33
Oh, the depth of the riches and wisdom and knowledge of God! How unsearchable are his judgments and how inscrutable his ways!

Think of an example: If I hold a pen in my hand, I can decide to drop it or not. I don't sit paralyzed, wondering, "Has God predestined for me to drop this pen?" I simply decide it, and I drop it (unless God intervenes in some special way). After I drop it, I can recognize the fact that God had planned for me to do it. That's the way everything is; God plans it, but we still live out each experience in the successive moments of time, making decisions.

Someone has said that the sovereignty of God and the responsibility of man are like two train rails going toward heaven; it seems to us like they will never meet, but when they get to heaven, where God understands everything, they come together.

For Review:

We can think of all events from two perspectives. What are they?

2. The Concept of Time

Let's look more carefully at the concept of time. It can help us accept the two-sided mystery of providence and freedom. Not *comprehend* it totally, but *accept* it. Have you ever thought about the relativity of time? Hypothetically, if you could observe an explosion on a planet four light years from the earth, when did the explosion happen? From your perspective, it just occurred, but from the perspective on that planet, it occurred four years ago. And if an explosion just happened on earth, from the perspective of a planet four light years away from you, it will not "happen" until four years from now. It all depends on your vantage point.

Einstein said, "The past, present and future are only illusions, even if stubborn ones."[21] Some scientists are now describing time more like a "block" instead of a line. Paul Davies, Australian physicist, says,

> The most straightforward conclusion is that both past and future are fixed. For this reason, physicists prefer to think of time as laid out in its entirety—a timescape, analogous to a landscape—with all past and future events located there together. It is a notion sometimes referred to as block time. Completely absent from this description of nature is anything that singles out a privileged special moment as the present or any process that would systematically turn future events into present, then past, events. In short, the time of the physicist does not pass or flow.[22]

---

[21] Quoted in Paul Davies, "That Mysterious Flow", *Scientific American*, September, 2002, p. 41.

[22] Paul Davies, "That Mysterious Flow," p. 42.

This is very interesting, especially when we think of how God sees time. From His eternal perspective beyond time, He sees all the moments interconnected. Time is not relative for God, since He is the final reference point for everything. He sees how it all fits together, past, present, and future. This gives new meaning to the verse we quoted above: "With the Lord a day is like a thousand years, and a thousand years are like a day." (2 Peter 3:8)

Man, however, is inserted into what seems like a linear timeline. We live moment to moment, making free decisions. But we can't change God's eternal plan.

Have you ever read a science fiction book or seen a movie about going back in time? When they go back, it seems like people can freely make decisions, but they can't change the future. For example, in "Back to the Future," the young man portrayed by Michael Fox goes back in time and watches his parents fall in love. If he does something to keep them from falling in love, he won't exist! This points to the profound truth that, just like the whole universe is physically interdependent, so are all the moments of history. All time is interconnected, and only God sees the whole picture.

I can't think of a better way to express this than the following pithy proverb:

Proverbs 16:9
The heart of man plans his way, but the LORD establishes his steps.

Conclusion

Fortunately, we don't have to understand this completely in order to live our lives. We are only required to trust God, do what He says, and leave the consequences up to Him. That's what it means to live by faith.

Deuteronomy 29:29
The secret things belong to the LORD our God, but the things revealed belong to us and to our sons forever, that we may observe all the words of this law.

To ask what percentage God does and what percentage I do is not really the right question. In one sense, God does 100% and I do 100%. That is, God controls everything 100%, but I should do 100% of what He tells me to do.

The story of Abraham's spiritual pilgrimage can help us understand what it means to live by faith. The Lord promised him a descendant, even in his old age (Genesis 15:1-6), but he and his wife became discouraged as the years passed without a child. As their faith weakened, they decided to take things into their own hands; Abram would have a child with Hagar, Sarai's Egyptian servant (Genesis 16:1-16). The child was called Ishmael, born when Abram was 86 years old. However, God appears again to Abraham (his new name) when he is 99 years old. He tells them that they have deviated from God's plan; Ishmael was not the promised heir. God promises that Abraham will have a child with Sarah (her new name), who was now 90 years old. This time, Abraham and Sarah trust God, and Isaac is born (Genesis 21:1-3). Next, we see how strong Abraham's faith has become, when he is willing to offer Isaac on the altar (Genesis 22). When our faith in God's sovereignty is weak, we tend to become anxious and take things in our own hands, leading often to disobey. When our faith is strong, we can harmonize God's sovereignty with our responsibility by doing what God says and leaving the results to Him.

There's a beautiful poem called "Footprints in the Sand." The author dreams that he is walking along the beach with the Lord and looks back over the path of his life. Usually there are two sets of footprints, but he is surprised to see only one set of footprints in certain sad and difficult moments. He turns to the Lord and asks why He was not with him in those moments. The Lord answers that in those moments, He was carrying him; those footprints were the Lord's![23] I would like to modify this encouraging idea slightly and add that God is carrying us *all the way*! During our whole life, we sense ourselves walking along the beach, but when we look back, we see only the Lord's footprints at every step.

For Review:

1. What's the difference between the way God sees time and the way man sees time?

2. How does the difference between the way God sees time and the way man sees time help us accept both the sovereignty of God and the freedom of man?

3. What does it mean to live by faith, harmonizing God's sovereignty with our responsibility?

---

[23] See <https://www.onlythebible.com/Poems/Footprints-in-the-Sand-Poem.html> (Feb. 16, 2024)

The Essential Point
God governs everything that happens, but man is free to make decisions and is responsible for his own actions.

For Personal Application

a) Bible Study

For your devotional time this week, read chapters 39-41 of Job.

Job wanted to know why he was suffering. These chapters give God's answer, but it is not exactly the kind of answer Job was looking for. Analyze for yourself the main point of these chapters and write your ideas in your notebook. What is God's answer? What does this mean for you?

b) Prayer

Use the words of Job 42:1-6 to guide your prayer time.

c) Memorization of Scripture

Proverbs 16:9
The heart of man plans his way, but the LORD establishes his steps.

For Further Reflection and Discussion

1. How does it help you to know God is in control? Can you share an experience when it helped you to think of the providence of God?

2. Does believing in the sovereignty of God tend to make you passive about some things? Explain how.

3. How would you answer someone who asks why we should pray if God already has everything planned?

4. How would it change your way of thinking and feeling if you believed that man does not really have freedom to make decisions?

6. Why Does God Allow Us to Suffer?

"My God, my God, why have you forsaken me?"

(Jesus on the cross, Mark 15.34)

Introduction

The famous existentialist philosopher Albert Camus once explained to a pastor in Paris,

> The silence of the universe has led me to conclude that the world is without meaning... Something is dreadfully wrong. I am a disillusioned and exhausted man. I have lost faith, lost hope, ever since the rise of Hitler.[24]

It's not hard to understand the sense of deception that Camus felt because of Hitler. This raises a question for believers as well. We can't say that God isn't powerful enough to avoid evil. Neither can we deny that He is a loving God. Yet, if we accept both of these truths, we inevitably ask why He permits evil.

Furthermore, this becomes personal when we have an accident, get sick, or when something tragic happens to someone in our family. We ask, "Why did the Lord permit this? Am I being punished? Have I done something to deserve this?" Most people at some point wonder why God allows bad things to happen, either as a philosophical question or as a personal one, probably both.

In this chapter, we will study the origin of evil and suffering, suggest answers to the question of why God allowed it, and see what God does to solve the problem. We will show that God turns everything into good, one of the most encouraging

---

[24] Howard Mumma, *Albert Camus and the Minister* (Brewster, Massachusetts: Paraclete Press, 2000), pp. 13-14.

teachings in the Bible, and review some of the ways He uses suffering in our lives.

A. Man Caused the Fall.

The first thing we need to establish is that man caused the Fall. God didn't force Adam and Eve to sin. God made them in His own image with freedom to make decisions; He didn't manipulate their minds or their wills, causing them to sin.

Imagine the Garden of Eden, where everyone and everything lived together in harmony. They only spoke kind words. They experienced no hurricanes or earthquakes, no sickness or pain, no sadness or anger. The insects didn't bite people. Dogs and cats played freely together, and the lions rested with the lambs. That's the way God made the world! It was not only good; it was *very* good! What a wonderful creation!

Genesis 1:31
God saw everything that he had made, and behold, it was very good.

But soon we read about the Fall, the disobedience of Adam and Eve, bringing the tragic corruption into creation (Genesis 3:6-10). The word *Fall* seems too weak to describe what happened in that instant. Genesis 3:7-19 describes the consequences of sin. Man hides from God and is afraid of Him. He is ashamed of himself. Adam blamed Eve, and Eve blamed the serpent. They suffer pain and work becomes tiring and tedious. Death is inevitable. In a word, sin brought conflict: between man and God, between man and other people, between man and nature, and between man and his own heart.

We have to start here. God isn't guilty for the evil that exists in the world. On the contrary, man himself is responsible!

B. Why Did God Allow the Fall?

But why did God allow the Fall? Why didn't God make man somehow unable to sin? Why did He give him freedom to obey or disobey? It's dangerous to speculate about the divine purposes, when the Bible doesn't reveal them clearly. However, there are some biblical concepts that might help. Let's start by asking how else God might have created man. If we try to imagine other scenarios, in which God somehow didn't permit evil, we encounter some serious problems. Eventually we arrive at the conclusion that this was the *best way*. I wouldn't say that God *had* to create man like this, but I think we can assume that He *wanted* to.

First, He wanted man to be in His own image. He wanted to make him even more astonishing than the plants and animals. This includes having the capacity to make decisions, to think his own thoughts, to exercise his own will and express his own emotions. These are the wonderful aspects of man, the results of an amazing supernatural act of creation.

Furthermore, He apparently didn't want obedience to be mechanical or forced, but voluntarily, from the heart. Notice that it was offensive to God when Satan suggested that Job was only faithful to Him because of the benefits he was receiving (Job 1:8-12). This shows that God desires our obedience to be motivated by love.

C.S. Lewis argues that God could have programmed man in such a way that his brain wouldn't function if he attempted to think something evil. He could have prevented suffering by constantly manipulating things. But these options would take away the meaning of free will.[25]

The final answer to the question of why God has allowed evil and suffering is that God does everything for His own glory. The plan of salvation brings Him glory. Jesus is a Savior, and he has been a Savior from eternity. His victory over sin and death reveals His true identity and His character.

These suggestions at least help us accept the fact that God has made the best plan. Other options would have meant that man was not really the image of God, that man's obedience would have been mechanical, and that God would not have fully displayed His glory.[26]

For Review:

1. Who is guilty of causing suffering?

2. What are the suggested answers for the question of why God has allowed evil and suffering?

3. Why did God make man with the freedom to disobey?

Now let's see how God governs the events of our lives to accomplish something good, even in suffering.

---

[25] C. S. Lewis, *The Problem of Pain* (New York: The Macmillan Company, 1962), 33-34. Originally published in 1940, it was his first apologetics book. A 2001 edition is available from HarperCollins.

[26] For more on this subject by the author, as well as an explanation of the arguments of C.S. Lewis and other apologists, see Richard B. Ramsay, *The Certainty of the Faith* (Phillipsburg, NJ: P&R Publishing, 2007).

C. God Turns Everything into Good.

When we are suffering, it helps to remember that the Lord is always seeking our good. Romans 8 is a key passage that develops this theme. Paul explains that God's purpose for Christians is that they become like His Son Jesus Christ. He does not promise material prosperity, nor earthly power, but spiritual blessing. All of our experiences help us grow spiritually.

Romans 8:28-30
And we know that for those who love God all things work together for good, for those who are called according to his purpose. For those whom he foreknew he also predestined to be conformed to the image of his Son, in order that he might be the firstborn among many brothers. And those whom he predestined he also called, and those whom he called he also justified, and those whom he justified he also glorified.

The argument is that, if God gave His own Son for us, there is no limit to what He will do for us!

Romans 8:31-32
What then shall we say to these things? If God is for us, who can be against us? He who did not spare his own Son but gave him up for us all, how will he not also with him graciously give us all things?

Paul concludes emphatically and poetically that there is nothing that can separate us from God's love. Read it slowly and prayerfully; it's such an encouraging passage!

Romans 8:37-39

No, in all these things we are more than conquerors through him who loved us. For I am sure that neither death nor life, nor angels nor rulers, nor things present nor things to come, nor powers, nor height nor depth, nor anything else in all creation, will be able to separate us from the love of God in Christ Jesus our Lord.

The point of this chapter depends on the point we just made in the previous chapter. If God does not govern everything that happens, then we could not trust Him to work all things out for our good. But if we know God is in control, it helps us to accept the negative experiences.

Sometimes we don't know exactly why God permits a certain problem, but at least we know that *He* knows why. That's the lesson we learn from the book of Job. Job was a righteous man, but God allowed Satan to afflict him, as a test of his faithfulness. He lost his possessions, his family, and his health. Job's friends tried to convince him that he had done something especially bad in order to deserve his tragedy. However, Job knew that wasn't the case and he wanted God to explain things to him. If we think about it, we can understand why God didn't want to tell him the reason he was suffering: precisely because it was a test. Suppose that God had told him, "Be patient! Wait a little longer! I'm trying to prove to Satan that you serve me because you love me, not because I have blessed you with prosperity!" It would have made things easier for Job, but it would have made the test invalid.

The Lord appears to Job at the end of the book (Job 38-41), but He doesn't answer Job's question the way he wanted. Instead, He asks Job some questions about nature. Where were you when I laid the foundations of the world? (38:4). Do you know where light comes from? (38:19). What does the Lord mean with these questions? He wants to put Job in his place and reorient the discussion. There are many things you don't understand, so why are you surprised that you don't understand your suffering? God was asking that he simply trust Him, without understanding everything. In other words, Job had to believe that God was both all-powerful and all-good at the same time.

In everything that happens to us there are multiple actors: God, Satan, ourselves, and other people, each with his or her own intentions. The Lord is always working for our good, and Satan is always working for our harm. All problems originated in the Garden of Eden, caused by sin, and since then, there has been a cosmic war between good and evil, and between God and Satan. God is governing all of history to eliminate evil, bring salvation, and restore harmony, but Satan is fighting in every moment to destroy God's purposes. In the meantime, we have to endure the tribulations with faith, knowing that God will make something very good out of it all.

The best example of how God directs everything for good is the death of Jesus. The event was at the same time terrible and wonderful! The wicked men who crucified Him committed the most horrible crime in history, but God directed in for our salvation!

When Jesus cried out, "My God, my God, why have you forsaken me?" (Mark 15:34), He was experiencing the agonizing separation from God the Father. He took all evil and all suffering upon Himself to solve the "problem of evil." He became like a "black hole" in the universe, pulling all evil and all suffering into His own soul.

2 Corinthians 5:21
For our sake he made him to be sin who knew no sin, so that in him we might become the righteousness of God.

135

If the Lord can turn such an evil event into something so good, what can He *not* turn into good?

For Review:

1. According to Romans 8, what is God's purpose in everything that happens to us? What does He do with our suffering?

2. What is the best example of how God turns everything into good?

D. Some Purposes of Suffering

Even though God often doesn't let us know the specific purpose of particular trials, He has explained in general some of the blessings He brings out of suffering. We can assume that when we hurt, it is probably for one of the following purposes:

1. It produces spiritual growth.

Romans 5:3-4
Not only that, but we rejoice in our sufferings, knowing that suffering produces endurance, and endurance produces character, and character produces hope.

James 1:2-4
Count it all joy, my brothers, when you meet trials of various kinds, for you know that the testing of your faith produces steadfastness. And let steadfastness have its full effect, that you may be perfect and complete, lacking in nothing.

2. It helps us understand and comfort others.

My father died when I was seventeen years old, and I am sure that this tragedy helped me understand others in their moment of pain. I know that in way they are in "shock," and what they most need is someone who can listen to them when they want to talk, maybe give them a hug, and probably take care of some of the details that will easily go unattended.

2 Corinthians 1:3-5
Blessed be the God and Father of our Lord Jesus Christ, the Father of mercies and God of all comfort, who comforts us in all our affliction, so that we may be able to comfort those who are in any affliction, with the comfort with which we ourselves are comforted by God. For as we share abundantly in Christ's sufferings, so through Christ we share abundantly in comfort too.

Somebody might object, "But if nobody suffered, nobody would need comforting! Wouldn't that be better yet?" I can only say that there is something profoundly important in learning to comfort other people. We become more like Christ when we do it, and we therefore experience something divine.

3. It might be a test.

Don't forget that our trials have consequences beyond life here on earth and beyond the realm of humans. There are heavenly witnesses that are observing everything, just as in the case of Job. When we resist a test, the angels also sing victory.

1 Peter 1:6-7
In this you rejoice, though now for a little while, if necessary, you have been grieved by various trials, so that the tested genuineness of your faith—more precious than gold that perishes though it is tested by fire—may be found to result in praise and glory and honor at the revelation of Jesus Christ.

4. Sometimes it is loving fatherly discipline.

I remember the times I had to be disciplined for disobeying my parents. It made me realize the importance of what I had done. I am also sure, although it was painful for me to do it as well as for them, that my children grew in character as a result of those moments when I disciplined them.

Hebrews 12:5-6
And have you forgotten the exhortation that addresses you as sons? "My son, do not regard lightly the discipline of the Lord, nor be weary when reproved by him. For the Lord disciplines the one he loves, and chastises every son whom he receives." (See also Proverbs 3:11-12)

Just as a good father disciplines his children at times, God also disciplines us. But it's important to distinguish between this kind of personal discipline and retributive or vengeful punishment. Judicial punishment, such as the government exercises on a criminal, is to make retribution, to make the criminal "pay" for his crime. On the other hand, the Lord's discipline of His children has a positive purpose, and it is motivated by love. When God disciplines us, He does not stop loving us. We can assume that it hurts Him to do it, but that He knows it is for our good.

E. How Should We React to Suffering?

The history of Joseph in Genesis illustrates how we should react to suffering, while recognizing the sovereignty of God. His brothers had betrayed him, selling him as a slave. Nevertheless, the Lord used Joseph in Egypt to store wheat and save the lives of many people during a famine, even the lives of his own family. After Joseph reveals himself to his brother, he says:

Genesis 50:20
As for you, you meant evil against me, but God meant it for good, to bring it about that many people should be kept alive, as they are today.

This verse expresses the duality that exists in everything that happens to us, and it reveals the secret of how we should react to suffering. On the one hand, we should recognize the bad side of the experience, and on the other hand, we should recognize the good side.

This means that if I break my leg, I don't have to pretend that it doesn't hurt or pretend that I am happy with the pain. Nevertheless, I can remind myself that the Lord has permitted it for some purpose and I can trust Him to turn it into a blessing. This is what makes the sovereignty of God such a wonderful doctrine! We can't lose! Whatever happens, He turns it into good!

Romans 8:31
What then shall we say to these things? If God is for us, who can be against us?

Romans 8:37
...In all these things we are more than conquerors through him who loved us.

We can apply this promise to our family and friends as well. When I lived in Santiago, Chile, I suffered mild fainting spells off and on for a few months. Once I was in the supermarket with Angelica, pushing the cart, and felt like I was going to fall to the floor. I held on tight and didn't fall, but I knew I needed to see a doctor. When he sent me for an electrocardiogram and a brain scan, I have to admit that I was nervous. I began to analyze the consequences of a possible serious illness. After a few days, I began to accept the fact that in a sense, I myself was ready to go. However, I couldn't quite accept the consequences for my family, especially my children. Nicolas was three, and Melany was only a year old. It hurt to think of them growing up without their father. The only comfort I found was in Romans 8:28:

Romans 8:28
And we know that for those who love God all things work together for good, for those who are called according to his purpose.

I had applied this verse to myself many times, but the new thing for me in this case was to apply it also to my family. If something were to happen to me, even though it was hard to understand, the Lord would also work this for their good somehow. I believe that the Lord permitted this time of meditation to teach me an important truth. Thankfully, the results of the exams showed nothing more than a bad case of sinusitis. Thankfully, I didn't have anything serious and I had learned a good lesson.

For Review:

What are the two aspects of an appropriate reaction to suffering?

The Essential Point

God turns all things into spiritual benefit for His people.

For Personal Application

a) Bible Study

This week, do a study of two examples of suffering that God turned into blessings. Read 2 Corinthians 12:7-10 and Philippians 1:12-14. Write down a description of the negative events and how God used them for something good.

b) Prayer

Read 1 Thessalonians 5:16-18 to guide your prayer time. Think about the problems that you are experiencing now. Give thanks to God for the fact that He will turn them into blessings.

c) Memorization of Scripture

Romans 8:28
And we know that for those who love God all things work together for good, for those who are called according to his purpose. (ESV)

For Further Reflection and Discussion:

1. Think of some example in your life when something bad happened to you, but God turned it into something good. Explain the experience.

2. Identify some ways in which you are suffering now and suggest some possible purposes that God might have in permitting them.

Conclusion

These chapters have analyzed subjects that are so complex that they require much more study and reflection than this brief study could cover. I hope that you will continue studying these issues for yourself. I trust that the result will be a stronger faith, greater joy, and a closer relationship with the Lord. May you continue persevering and growing in grace!

All The "Essential Points"

Chapter 1
1. We are justified and sanctified by grace through faith.
2. True faith will produce a changed life with good works.
3. Once saved, we will not lose our salvation.

Chapter 2
1. Every Christian has the Holy Spirit upon conversion, and every Christian has spiritual gifts.
2. We should concern ourselves especially with growing in the fruit of the Spirit, becoming "full" of the Spirit.
3. We also may be "filled" with the Spirit on special occasions to carry out a special ministry.

Chapter 3
We no longer keep the ceremonial and civil aspects of the Old Testament law in the same way as before Christ, but we do keep the moral aspect.

Chapter 4
1. Avoid the pitfalls of legalism and libertinism.
2. Use the means of grace and practice repentance.
3. Keep your eyes on Jesus and live like children of God.

Chapter 5
God governs everything that happens, but man is free to make decisions and is responsible for his own actions.

Chapter 6
God turns all things into spiritual benefit for His people.

www.ingramcontent.com/pod-product-compliance
Lightning Source LLC
Chambersburg PA
CBHW071626140626
46555CB00021B/525